IN THE
NATIONAL INTEREST

General Sir John Monash once exhorted a graduating class to 'equip yourself for life, not solely for your own benefit but for the benefit of the whole community'. At the university established in his name, we repeat this statement to our own graduating classes, to acknowledge how important it is that common or public good flows from education.

Universities spread and build on the knowledge they acquire through scholarship in many ways, well beyond the transmission of this learning through education. It is a necessary part of a university's role to debate its findings, not only with other researchers and scholars, but also with the broader community in which it resides.

Publishing for the benefit of society is an important part of a university's commitment to free intellectual inquiry. A university provides civil space for such inquiry by its scholars, as well as for investigations by public intellectuals and expert practitioners.

This series, In the National Interest, embodies Monash University's mission to extend knowledge and encourage informed debate about matters of great significance to Australia's future.

Professor Margaret Gardner AC
President and Vice-Chancellor,
Monash University

GARETH EVANS

GOOD INTERNATIONAL CITIZENSHIP: THE CASE FOR DECENCY

MONASH
UNIVERSITY
PUBLISHING

Good International Citizenship: The Case for Decency
© Copyright 2022 Gareth Evans
All rights reserved. Apart from any uses permitted by Australia's *Copyright Act 1968*, no part of this book may be reproduced by any process without prior written permission from the copyright owners. Inquiries should be directed to the publisher.

Monash University Publishing
Matheson Library Annexe
40 Exhibition Walk
Monash University
Clayton, Victoria 3800, Australia
https://publishing.monash.edu

Monash University Publishing brings to the world publications which advance the best traditions of humane and enlightened thought.

ISBN: 9781922464972 (paperback)
ISBN: 9781922464996 (ebook)

Series: In the National Interest
Editor: Louise Adler
Project manager & copyeditor: Paul Smitz
Designer: Peter Long
Typesetter: Cannon Typesetting
Proofreader: Gillian Armitage
Printed in Australia by Ligare Book Printers

A catalogue record for this book is available from the National Library of Australia.

The paper this book is printed on is in accordance with the standards of the Forest Stewardship Council®. The FSC® promotes environmentally responsible, socially beneficial and economically viable management of the world's forests.

GOOD INTERNATIONAL CITIZENSHIP

For a state to be a good international citizen means, above all else, caring about other people's suffering and doing everything reasonably possible to prevent and alleviate it. States that earn that description are those seen to be seriously committed to helping others, even when there is no direct or obvious security or economic benefit to themselves to be derived from doing so—in areas such as humanitarian relief and development assistance, human rights and environmental protection, arms control, peacemaking and peacekeeping.

Being generally seen to be a good international citizen is a mantle hard won. Many countries have acted generously and selflessly in particular contexts at particular times— for example, with disaster relief in response to earthquakes and other natural catastrophes, or providing peacekeepers in response to particular conflicts, or initiating particular arms-control movements. But not many have acted so consistently, in so many different contexts, over so many years, under enough different governments, as to be widely seen as *natural* good international citizens. Those who most often have so acted, and have been warmly regarded by the wider world accordingly, have been the Scandinavians— Sweden and Norway especially—with Canada and New Zealand not far behind.

Australia likes to think of itself in that company, and from time to time has deserved to be so regarded. But only from time to time. As will be described in the pages that follow, our overall record has been patchy at best, lamentable at worst, and is presently embarrassingly poor. It is time to take stock of why it matters to be, and be seen to be, a good international citizen; how and why we have been backsliding; and what we can do as a nation to restore our credentials.

The concept of good international citizenship described in this essay—its pursuit not only a moral imperative but a hard-headed national interest in its own right—was first developed by me in a series of speeches after I became Australia's foreign minister in 1988,[1] and became one of the central guiding pillars of our foreign policy for the remaining eight years of the Hawke and Keating Labor governments. It was then explicitly rejected, like so much else of our liberal internationalist foreign policy, by Alexander Downer and the Howard Coalition government which followed. Its 1997 foreign policy white paper, 'In the National Interest', reverted to the traditional duo of security and economic interests, completely abandoning the concept of good international citizenship as a third category of interest in its own right, while restoring as a separate objective the pursuit of 'national values', described as reflecting our 'predominantly European intellectual and cultural heritage'. Good international citizenship language was resurrected by the Rudd and Gillard Labor governments of 2007 to 2013, and when Tony Abbott became prime minister he occasionally borrowed the phrase—he liked three-word mantras—but not its content. But under the subsequent Coalition governments of Turnbull and Morrison, it just dropped out of sight—neither embraced nor disavowed, but simply ignored.

The description of universally minded *individuals* as 'global citizens' has been around forever, with the Greek philosopher Diogenes saying as early as 412 BCE 'I am a citizen of the world', and the Dutch scholar Erasmus equally famously saying in 1522 that he would like to be. The identification of activist role models as global citizens, and programs of 'education for global citizenship', have become quite popular in recent times.[2] But it is not at all usual to describe *states* in these terms. I don't claim to have invented the terminology in this context. It has obvious rhetorical appeal, and a Canadian governor-general is on record in 1967 describing his country as a 'good international citizen'.[3] No doubt other such quotes can be found. But insofar as there has been recognition in the international academic literature of the concept of good international citizenship—and, in particular, the idea of its pursuit by a state being a core national *interest*, not just a value—this has been squarely attributed to its embrace in Australia by the Hawke and Keating governments.[4] In that literature the concept has been generally warmly received, and seen as a model worth following elsewhere in the world. But it cannot be pretended that it has yet gained much traction with other governments. For reasons which I hope will become clear in the following pages, I believe it deserves to.

There is no standard, agreed definition of good international citizenship, and opinions will vary as to the best ways of assessing national performance. An obvious conceptual starting point is the Charter of the United Nations, which clearly states the new global organisation's four defining objectives as peace and security ('to save succeeding generations from the scourge of war'), human rights ('to reaffirm faith in fundamental human rights, in the dignity and worth of the human person, in the equal rights of men and women'), international law ('justice and respect for the obligations arising from … international law') and development ('to promote social progress and better standards in larger freedom').

An outstanding contribution to translating these broad themes into specific operational benchmarks has been made by Sydney University's Dr Alison Pert in her 2014 book *Australia as a Good International Citizen*. She focuses on two big themes, each of them with a great many sub-themes: international law (encompassing both compliance with existing law and commitment to improving its content) and multilateralism (encompassing participation in international institutions like the UN and G20, overseas aid performance, and visible commitment to cooperative multilateral problem-solving more generally). A more recent analysis by her Sydney colleague Gabriele Abbondanza, in a comprehensive journal review of the literature on the subject, applies a five-part definitional framework: respect for international law, multilateralism, pursuit of humanitarian and idealist objectives, active support for the rules-based order, and 'a congruous identity matched by consistent domestic policies'.[5] These are rich, complex and nuanced analyses, but perhaps a little too abstract, and legally focused, for easy non-scholarly communication and acceptance.

My own instinct, embracing most of the substance of these analyses but distilling it in a different way, is that there are four big practical benchmarks which matter above all else when one is assessing Australia's record, or that of any other country, as a good international citizen:

- being a generous aid donor, supporting as best we can countries and peoples much less well off than ourselves;
- doing everything we can to protect and advance universally recognised human rights—those enshrined in those great post–World War II charters, the Universal Declaration of Human Rights, the International Covenant on Civil and Political Rights, and the International Covenant on Economic, Social and Cultural Rights;
- doing everything we reasonably can to achieve international peace and security, to prevent the horror and misery of war and mass atrocity crimes, and to alleviate their consequences, including for refugees fleeing their impact; and
- being an actively committed participant in collaborative and cooperative attempts to solve the biggest of all collective-action problems: the great existential risks

posed by health pandemics, global warming and nuclear war.

Australia's performance against all of these benchmarks—not nearly as good as it could and should be—is discussed in some detail in following sections.[6]

But to begin at the beginning: why does all this matter? Why should we, not just in Australia but *any* country, care about poverty, human rights atrocities, health epidemics, environmental catastrophes, weapons proliferation or any other problems afflicting people in faraway countries when they do not, as is often the case, have any direct or immediate impact on our own security or prosperity? Should Australians care about terrorist atrocities in the Middle East only because extreme jihadist movements seek to recruit deluded young men who may return to threaten our homeland security? Should we care about Ebola outbreaks in West Africa only because the disease might turn up here? Should we care about refugees from Afghanistan and Iran and Sri Lanka only because they might become queue-jumping asylum seekers threatening our territorial integrity by arriving by boat? Should Australians care about the catastrophic humanitarian risks of any nuclear weapons exchange only if radiation-cloud or nuclear-winter impacts are likely to reach our own shores?

Isn't all this just boy-scout stuff, not the real business of national government? What has it got to do with what any country should *really* care about—advancing and protecting its national interests? These questions are often asked by self-described political realists, and they have to be answered. My own answer, which I hope will be seen as compelling, is that we have both a moral imperative *and* a national interest imperative to be, and be seen to be, a good international citizen.

THE MORAL IMPERATIVE

At the heart of the case for good international citizenship is simply that this is the right thing to do—that states, like individuals, have a moral obligation to do the least harm, and the most good, they can do. Answers will vary, depending on one's philosophical or spiritual bent, as to what is the source of that obligation. But the striking thing is just how much convergence there is around basic principles, whether one's approach to ethics is religiously or humanistically based, and whatever the cultural tradition in which one has been brought up. In the words of the British philosopher Derek Parfit, defenders of different approaches to moral reasoning are 'climbing the same mountain on different sides'.[7]

The evolution of my own thinking on these issues, for what it's worth, reflects that reality. In my early Sunday school years, Christ's 'golden rule' command to 'do unto others what you would have them do unto you' seemed a complete and compelling answer, as variations on it continue to be in so many other religious cultures. As I grew older, and my belief in a deity who could possibly be, simultaneously, all-powerful, all-knowing and all-good evaporated, I went looking for moral guideposts based on secular argument rather than divine direction.

The first I encountered, in my undergraduate days at Melbourne University, was from my philosophy lecturer HJ McCloskey, who took the robust view that moral principles are self-evident truths, discoverable simply by intuition. My contemporaries will probably recall him as vividly as I still do, booming with great deliberation, conviction and gravity: 'The rich man has a duty to help the poor man.' Well yes, but wasn't there more to it than that?

Other philosophical traditions to which I was then exposed, at Melbourne and later at Oxford, did indeed seem to put more meat on the bones. One was the duty-based (or deontological) branch of ethics originating in the eighteenth century with Immanuel Kant's 'categorical imperatives': 'Act only according to that maxim by which you can also will that it would become a universal law' and 'Act in such a way that you always treat humanity, whether in your own person or in the person of any other, never simply as a means, but always at the same time as an end'. Although reason rather than divine-authority derived, these prescriptions have essentially the same flavour as the Christian golden rule (although Kant himself always resisted that connection), and accordingly have an instinctive universal appeal.

What had a much more immediate impact on my own thinking—not least because their works were a lot easier to read!—was the utilitarianism espoused by the nineteenth-century British philosophers Jeremy Bentham and John Stuart Mill: do that which contributes to the greatest happiness of the greatest number, do intervene to prevent harm to others, but don't be paternalistic about curbing individual behaviour which infringes the rights of no-one else. The whole philosophical tradition of consequentialism which has developed from this— assessing the morality of actions by their consequences for the wellbeing of others—is a hugely helpful guide to decent policymaking. My Melbourne University contemporary Peter Singer, recognised globally as the pre-eminent utilitarian philosopher of his time, has shown this in his innumerable thoughtful contributions to public debate on everything from animal rights to global governance.[8]

That said, in the real world of policymaking, it is all too common to find starkly competing claims of rights or freedoms, and the trick is always to strike a balance between them in a way that has some readily explicable principled foundation. It is not always easy to reconcile individual or minority group claims of right with the happiness of the greatest number—majorities can indeed be tyrannical, and very much enjoy their tyranny. In my own ministerial and other public policy roles, I have often found it helpful, accordingly, to view policy dilemmas through a wider than just utilitarian lens, in particular John Rawls's contractarian model of social justice. Rawls, probably the most influential of all twentieth-century ethics theorists, argues in his seminal 1971 work *A Theory of Justice* that social rules should be made on the basis of what would be rationally negotiated if you were designing a new society but ignorant of the place you will occupy in it. If you don't know whether you will have black skin or white skin, for example, you will hardly agree to any arrangements whereby one or the other will secure you advantages of class, status or power.

The main ethical traditions I have sketched here do not necessarily produce precisely the same answer to every practical problem to which one might seek to apply them. But the reality remains that they are all intuitively, emotionally or rationally attractive, and all point in essentially the same direction: demanding respect for our common humanity.[9] Whatever may be our differences in terms of nationality, race, ethnicity, religion, language, caste, class or ideology, what we have in common is our status as sentient human beings: living, breathing, feeling human beings who can experience pain and suffering and humiliation, and who deserve to have our dignity as human beings equally respected.

Recognition of our common humanity means that people should be treated not on the basis of what we *are* as a result of our genes, or where we were born, or the circumstances of our upbringing, but on the basis of what we *do*, and above all on the decency or not with which we behave towards our fellow human beings. And when it comes to how we are treated and how we behave, what is true for individuals in our local and national communities is also true for whole countries in the global community. Recognition of, and respect for, our common humanity is the moral core of the concept of good international citizenship.

THE NATIONAL INTEREST IMPERATIVE

Of course, it is the primary business of any country's foreign policy to advance and protect the national interest: we should be neither naïve nor defensive about this. But foreign policymakers, and those in the media and elsewhere who influence them, far too often still think of national interests *only* in terms of the familiar duo of security and prosperity: geopolitical, strategic and physical security-related interests on the one hand, and trade, investment and prosperity-related interests on the other.

This does not mean they have ignored entirely some of the core business of what I describe as good international citizenship—mass atrocity crimes, poverty, disease, the grinding misery of displacement, the awful human cost of natural disasters, or the risk of deadly conflict in faraway places. Sometimes governments do make commitments which cannot easily be characterised as advancing the traditional security–prosperity duo, and explain them in terms of meeting international legal obligations, or responding to requests from allies and friends, or—indeed—as *value* issues, where you are taking action just because it is the morally right thing to do. It is not in fact unusual for Australian governments, like others, to act in a value-driven way—not least in offering relief in response to natural disasters like tidal waves in Aceh, cyclones in the Pacific or earthquakes in Nepal. And in doing so they will often find themselves reflecting genuine community sentiment. Australians are certainly as compassionate as anyone else in the world when their attention is engaged on humanitarian issues.

But the trouble is that most of the time when governments, both Australian and others, do act in this way, their actions are seen, by themselves as well as others, as discretionary add-ons—not as engaging in the core, hard-headed business of foreign policy. These issues are simply not given the same kind of priority as the advancement and protection of the traditional security–prosperity duo. This has wider implications for effective foreign policymaking. If governments do not think of these responses as core foreign policy business, fitting squarely, when properly understood, within a national interests rather than just values-based framework, they get increasingly drawn into the kind of adhocery which has characterised the conduct, on both the Coalition and Labor sides, of so much of Australia's international relations as well as domestic policy in recent years. Too much decision-making has lacked shape and coherence, lurching erratically from one position to another, and picking up and dropping aid commitments, or treaty negotiation commitments, or principled positions on policy issues like climate change, as the domestic mood is perceived to change.

If decent international behaviour, of the kind I am describing as good international citizenship, is simply some kind of charitable impulse, the reality is that in our political culture—like that of many others—this is an impulse that will often have difficulty surviving the rigours of domestic political debate. For both major parties, far too much current foreign policymaking is wet-finger-in-the-air stuff, driven by domestic political priorities. More attention is paid to the perceived messages of opinion polls and focus groups, and to the sometimes idiosyncratic predilections and prejudices of party leaders—rather too many of whom, when they assume that role, seem to find international issues terra incognita—than intelligent analysis and systematic priority setting. Politics is a cynical, as well as bloody and dangerous, trade. And it is a business often with very limited tolerance for embracing what cannot be described in hard-headed national interest terms.

All this makes the case for seeing good international citizenship through not only a moral but a national interest lens. I have long argued, accordingly—including throughout my term as foreign minister—that instead of conceptualising national interests just in terms of the two familiar boxes of security and prosperity, we need to think in terms of every country having a *third* national interest: being, and being seen to be, a good international citizen. My point has been that the returns from good, selfless international behaviour are more than just warm inner glows: that such behaviour can generate hard-headed, practical national advantage of the kind that appeals to realists—and political cynics—as well as idealists. I have wanted, in short, to somehow square the circle between realists and idealists, by finding a way of making the point that idealism could in fact be realistic.

There are three kinds of hard-headed return for a state being, and being seen to be, a good international citizen.

The first is *progress on issues requiring collective international action* which might not otherwise be achievable. Good international citizenship requires, almost by definition, a cooperative mindset—being willing to engage in collective international action to advance global and regional public goods. Putting it another way, this means helping to resolve what former UN secretary-general

Kofi Annan used to describe as 'problems without passports': those which are by their nature beyond the capacity of any one state, however powerful, to individually solve. The list of issues requiring such multilateral diplomacy is familiar, covering a large proportion of what I describe in this essay as benchmark issues for assessing good international citizenship performance. They include bringing global warming under control, and achieving a world free of health pandemics, out-of-control cross-border population flows, international trafficking of drugs and people, and extreme poverty; a world without cross-border terrorism; and a world on its way to abolishing all weapons of mass destruction.

For states like Australia, being willing to participate actively in such collective problem-solving does not—given the number of factors always involved, and their complexity—guarantee that solutions will actually be found, and that we will always benefit directly from them in security or economic terms. But while good international citizenship might not be a sufficient condition for such success, it is a necessary one, in the sense that collective-action problems will never be solved without enough states bringing a collective-action mindset to them.

The second return from good international citizenship is *reciprocity*. Foreign policymakers are no more immune to ordinary human instincts than anyone else, and if I take your problems seriously, you are that much more likely to help me solve mine. My help for you today in solving your terrorism problem or environmental problem or piracy problem might reasonably lead you to be more willing than you might otherwise be to help solve my people- or drug-trafficking problem tomorrow. And our help in meeting your priority development assistance needs might not be entirely unrelated to your willingness to support our candidacy for a UN committee or key international post. The reciprocity involved is not always explicit or transparent, and subtlety will often be an advantage in achieving it. But no practising diplomat will be unaware of the reality, and utility, of this dynamic, and no government policymaker should be oblivious to it.

The third return, more intangible but perhaps most significant overall, is *reputational*. A country's general image, how it projects itself—its culture, its values, its policies—and how in turn it is seen by others, is of fundamental importance in determining how well it succeeds in advancing and protecting its traditional national interests. Over many decades of active international engagement I have witnessed, over and again, how this matters. It matters in determining whether one is seen as a good country to invest in and trade with, to visit, to study in, and to trust in security terms. And it matters in being seen as a good country to support for responsible international positions and in responsible decision-making forums, and as one good to work with in solving those transnational issues that are beyond the capacity of any country to solve by itself. To be, and be seen to be, a good international citizen, in all the ways described in these pages, is a key element of what Harvard political scientist Joseph Nye has famously described as a state's 'soft power'. Such power derives from a combination of foreign policies (when they are seen as legitimate and having moral authority), political values (when the state is seen to live up to them, both at home and abroad) and culture (where it is attractive to others).[10]

Having the kind of reputation which generates soft power is particularly important for middle powers like Australia, those who are by no means insignificant in the global scheme of things, but are never going to be big enough and strong enough militarily or economically to demand that our interests be accommodated. We have to depend, rather, on our capacity to persuade, and to work cooperatively and constructively with others. In international diplomacy, as in life itself, the keys to being persuasive, and to working cooperatively and constructively, are being seen to be inherently decent. Being seen to be empathetic. Being seen to understand and be willing to accommodate the interests and values of others to the maximum extent possible. And being seen to be constantly searching for common ground, rather than just standing selfishly and defiantly and unthinkingly on one's own.

One example I have often used of a state's good international citizenship generating very traditional national interest returns is Sweden. Its well-deserved squeaky-clean reputation, developed over many decades, for aid generosity, human rights promotion, opposition to weapons of mass destruction, peacekeeping contributions and the like, has helped it to be, for many decades, a leading world supplier of conventional weapons, through firms like Bofors, Kockums and Saab. Sweden is not a country with whom anyone is reluctant to do business.

For some, this argument takes pragmatism a step too far. I think of the *Foreign Policy* interviewer who asked me some years ago: 'Don't you find it ironic that the example that comes to mind to justify the benefits of good international citizenship is the prospect of competitive advantage to the arms trade?' To which my answer then, as it would still be now, was this: 'I'm being deliberately ironic because I want to make the point, very strongly, that good international citizenship is not just the equivalent of boy-scout good deeds. What you need to be able to do is translate the kind of values that might be cherished by those of us who are boy scouts at heart into the hard-edged vocabulary of political discourse.'[11]

It is inevitable that the primary appeal of the concept of good international citizenship will be to idealists, those who don't need additional arguments to be persuaded that good foreign policy must extend to 'purposes beyond ourselves', to employ that wonderful phrase of the great Australian international relations theorist Hedley Bull. But, properly understood, it should be equally attractive to the most hard-headed of realists. Focusing on the benefits to traditional national security and economic interests that will flow from systematically pursuing good international citizenship objectives will be crucial in convincing less idealistically inclined audiences, in the wider community but especially in government itself. It will be crucial in persuading them that such pursuit is not a fringe activity best left to missionaries and the naïve, but rather something that every state worth the name should be doing, and by which it will be judged by the rest of the world, and by which its citizens will directly benefit if it gets it right.

AUSTRALIA'S RECORD: OVERSEAS AID

Being a generous aid donor—supporting as best one can countries and peoples much less well off than oneself— is the first of the four big practical benchmarks argued in this essay to be most helpful in assessing any country's record as a good international citizen. Australia once had credible claims to pass this test, but no longer. As aid givers, we are now very poor international citizens indeed.

The international target for overseas development assistance (ODA) as a proportion of gross national income (GNI) has long been 0.7 per cent, or 70 cents in every $100 the nation earns.[12] This is a target now met or exceeded by a number of countries with whom we like to compare ourselves, like Norway, Sweden, Denmark and the United Kingdom, and a goal that is regularly approached by a number of others, including Germany, the Netherlands and Switzerland. Australia's contribution, by contrast, now hovers around just 0.2 per cent—a pitiful 20 cents for every $100 of national income.

On 2020 figures, Australia now ranks twenty-first, down from ninth in 1995, among the thirty members of the OECD's Development Assistance Committee (some of whom are relatively poor but committed to following good governance guidelines in the assistance they do give). Of the twenty-two richer OECD donor countries against whom our performance is usually compared, only two—the United States and Portugal—are now less generous than Australia. And we were the worst performed of *any* rich-country donor in terms of the decline in our generosity over the last five decades. While of course it is not only the quantity but the quality of any country's development assistance that matters, there is nothing to suggest that there is anything so distinctively good about our aid that this could possibly compensate for its limited, and now further declining, amount. In global terms, Australia's aid performance has never been worse.[13]

While never spectacular, our record in the past has been less embarrassing.[14] In Australia, as elsewhere, ODA programs were practically unknown before World War II, but we started well enough in the 1950s with the Colombo Plan—giving money, goods and technical support to countries across South and South-East Asia—and providing significant support for the then colonies of Papua and New Guinea. The OECD database shows these programs averaging more than 0.5 per cent of GNI through the 1960s, and reaching a high of 0.65 per cent under the Whitlam government of 1972–75. While subsequent analysis has shown these figures to be significantly inflated and in need of correction as a result of data failings, it remains the case that we were throughout this period among the three or four most generous aid donors. Our generosity during the Robert Menzies era was more than twice as great as it is now under his current Coalition successor.[15]

Our performance started to diminish during the Fraser years from 1975 to 1983, and this continued into the early years of the Hawke government. On OECD figures, the proportion of ODA to GNI was 0.43 per cent in 1983–84, and had declined further to 0.33 per cent by the time I became foreign minister in 1988. I had an almighty struggle to keep it at that, with the Hawke–Keating governments' Expenditure Review Committee invariably wanting to cut aid rather than increase it to anywhere near the international gold standard of 0.7 per cent of GNI. Bill Hayden, foreign minister from 1983 to 1988, had been readily persuaded to slash our commitment to help meet government expenditure-reduction targets, clearly wearing his cooperative-former-treasurer's hat far more enthusiastically than his current international relations one. (Along the way, in 1986, he broke a $10 million recent treaty commitment to Papua New Guinea—which I, then responsible for resources and energy but also wearing the hat of minister assisting the foreign minister, was given the unenviable task of flying to Port Moresby to explain: one of the few times my colleague seemed to really enjoy having me share his portfolio.) As foreign minister myself, I was able to hold the line at close to the 0.33 per cent level for nearly eight years, until Labor left office in 1996, but not—to my deep regret—to do any better.

As unsatisfactory as things were then, they were to get considerably worse. The Howard government, for whom 'the single objective of Australia's aid program is ... to advance our national interests',[16] and for whom, as noted earlier, 'national interests' most definitely did not include good international citizenship, had no hesitation in further reducing our aid commitment, down to

0.24 per cent by 2004. The need to respond generously to Indonesia's Aceh tsunami catastrophe, and a deteriorating security and governance situation in Papua New Guinea, led to a reversal of that trend in the Howard government's remaining years. And with the Rudd and Gillard Labor governments committed to raising the level to at least 0.5 per cent, aid expenditure from 2007 to 2013 did come back to mid-1990s levels. But since 2013–14 it has fallen again, faster than it was scaled up, with successive cuts in real terms to the point where, by 2021–22, it had plunged back to 0.21 per cent.

The Morrison government announced in 2018 that it would freeze overseas aid in subsequent budgets at $4 billion—itself a figure down by nearly a third since the last Labor budget in 2013. In its 2020 and 2021 budgets, while keeping this headline figure unchanged, it in fact increased ODA by several hundred million dollars to meet COVID-19 pandemic needs among our Pacific island neighbours. But, in an interesting commentary on its mindset that there was more political risk than reward in being seen to be increasing the aid budget, the government refused to describe the increases in these terms, saying when pressed that they were 'temporary and targeted initiatives'. In any event, even taking these variations into account, the ANU's Stephen Howes calculates that, on currently available data and government forecasts, Australia's ODA commitment will drop to 0.19 per cent of GNI in 2023–24 and an even more lamentable 0.18 in 2024–25.[17]

The biggest problem in arguing for foreign aid, and the main reason why so many of our governments have been insouciant about cutting it, is that it is not generally seen by the political class and senior public service as a core national interest. There are some exceptions to that, as when the present government recently decided, as just noted, to increase aid to a number of Pacific island countries—clearly not just for good neighbourly reasons but to counter what was seen as China's increasing influence in the region, and to help avert the pandemic getting out of control, particularly in PNG, uncomfortably close to our border.

But most of the time, providing, or not providing, overseas aid is not seen as something that directly and immediately affects our national security or our national prosperity. It is seen as neither a geopolitical interest nor an economic interest. It's an optional extra. Helping poor countries to lift their people out of poverty may be a morally attractive thing to do, but this is seen as boy-scout territory, not the hard-headed pursuit of real national interests. In aid policy, the bean-counters—as I, like my predecessors and successors, found in government—will always demand that something less sentimental than a generalised sense of moral obligation be advanced to justify major expenditure.

My basic strategy in response, as foreign minister, was to try to satisfy the hard-heads by pointing to the Australian national interests, starting with the traditional duo of economic and security interests, that would be tangibly advanced by aid programs. In economic terms, giving scholarships directly benefits our education providers; supplying goods and services in support of poverty or public health or governance programs can directly benefit national contractors; and poverty alleviation and growth promotion strategies may work indirectly to increase trade. In security terms, public health strategies can work directly to stop the spread of infectious diseases to our shores, and poverty reduction strategies can serve our interests indirectly by helping to prevent uncontrolled, economically driven migration flows. Governance, rule of law and human rights protection strategies can also serve our security interests indirectly to the extent that they avoid state failure, and in turn the conflict-driven refugee outflows and terrorist-breeding potential associated with that.

But not everything I wanted to do could easily be justified in terms of traditional national interest priorities. The reality is that the world's more generous aid donors do not confine their support to programs where they are likely to directly and visibly benefit national security or prosperity. Nor should Australia. We should be supporting poverty alleviation programs in West Africa, or earthquake disaster relief in Haiti, simply for their own sake, because we can afford it, and it is the right thing to do. But while these arguments had some traction in the Cabinet room, I usually found it more helpful in budgetary negotiations to be able to make the point that so acting burnished our good international citizen credentials, winning us, over time, reputational and reciprocity returns—even if only voting support for seats on influential international policymaking bodies.

All that said, Australia remains on any view one of the richest countries in the world—twelfth or thirteenth in the world in the latest IMF and World Bank nominal GDP rankings. We can afford to be much more altruistic than we have been in assisting through really substantial aid programs the economic and social development of those many countries still struggling with poverty or national calamity. Moreover, there is reason to believe that ordinary Australians are considerably more willing to support that altruism—as both a moral and national interest imperative—than the more cynical of their governments have tended to assume. This is a theme addressed in the last section of this essay, which explores the politics of decency.

AUSTRALIA'S RECORD: HUMAN RIGHTS

The second benchmark to be applied in assessing whether any state deserves to be regarded as a good international citizen is whether it does everything it can to protect and advance the rights enshrined in the Universal Declaration of Human Rights, the International Covenant on Civil and Political Rights, and the International Covenant on Economic, Social and Cultural Rights. These are universally recognised standard-setters in principle, whatever shortfalls there may continue to be in their practical implementation. My focus in this context will be on civil and political rights like free association, non-discrimination on racial grounds, and legal due process. These are readily deliverable in any state if it has the necessary political will, in contrast with economic and other rights, the achievement of which often depend on other factors beyond a state's control, like natural resource availability.

The relevant standard here has to be *universal* values. To focus inwardly, as many politicians (not just conservatives) here and abroad prefer to do, on 'Australian values' or 'US values' or the like—with the implication being that these involve a rather superior brand of morality—is just too self-satisfied for words, and is not likely to generate much international reputational return.

In assessing good citizenship performance against universally accepted human rights standards, what counts is both external and internal behaviour. Looking outwards, this means supporting the development and institutionalisation of human rights values, and encouraging other countries to live up to them. Looking inwards, it means both complying with international human rights law, and doing everything possible to further improve domestic respect for, and enjoyment of, human rights. The two dimensions are inextricable. What happens at home does very much matter abroad: nobody likes those who do not practise what they preach.

Against these international standards, Australia's human rights record, both internally and externally, has been at best mixed.[18]

Looking Inward

We started well enough, at least on paper, in the post–World War II period with Evatt at the United Nations, and the Chifley Labor government, actively embracing the new international human rights charters. But at home the White Australia immigration policy, dating back to the birth of the Commonwealth, remained in full force for two more decades, and it was not, again, until the 1960s that systematic discrimination against Aboriginal and Torres Strait Islander peoples—including in the Constitution itself—began to be addressed. The attempt by the Menzies government to outlaw the Communist Party was quashed by the High Court in 1951, but the case turned on narrow technical issues and not on any kind of acknowledged recognition of a constitutional or other legal right to freedom of association. The absence of a national Bill of Rights in any form (an issue on which I have to concede the spectacular failure of my own advocacy, both in and out of government, over many years) continues to this day. This distinguishes us from every other country in the English-speaking world and beyond with whom we like to compare ourselves. And that is not a matter for national pride.

Some significant domestic steps forward were taken by the Whitlam government in the early 1970s, notably ending capital punishment for federal offences, passing the *Racial Discrimination Act*, finally dismantling the White Australia policy, and signing up to a series of international covenants and conventions which laid the foundations (through the external affairs power in the Constitution) for further human rights protection legislation otherwise beyond the Commonwealth's capacity to enact. But its creativity was stymied by Coalition opposition in the Senate. And the following Fraser government of 1975–83—while behaving admirably on refugee issues (a topic discussed later in this essay)—had no enthusiasm for any such adventures of its own.

The Hawke–Keating governments picked up a number of these pieces, especially with the passage of the *Sex Discrimination Act* and the creation of the Human Rights and Equal Opportunity Commission, but met familiar Senate and wider political obstacles in trying to enact a national Bill of Rights. Arguably our proudest domestic human rights achievements, although still leaving too much unfinished business, were in relation to Indigenous affairs. Symbolically, with Paul Keating's majestic Redfern speech in 1992: '… it was we who did the dispossessing … It was our ignorance and prejudice. And our failure to imagine these things being done to us.' And substantively, with the passage of the transformative *Native Title Act* the following year, implementing the High Court's historic Mabo decision—against relentless Coalition hostility (which, inter alia, kept me on my feet in the Senate for some fifty hours).

The Howard government's eleven years in office can most kindly be described as a period of total desolation for domestic human rights—not least on Indigenous issues, with 'black armband' history condemned, the Stolen Generations report rejected, native title sought to be diminished, and Pauline Hanson's overt racism accommodated. There was a renewed surge of human rights activism under the Rudd and Gillard governments of 2007–13, beginning with Kevin Rudd's deeply moving parliamentary apology to the Stolen Generations: '… for the indignity and degradation thus inflicted on a proud people and a proud culture, we say sorry.' There was over-due re-engagement with UN treaties and treaty bodies, same-sex couples received legislative protection, and Julia Gillard was a fiercely effective defender of gender equality. But, as will be discussed in the next section, the treatment of asylum seekers during this Labor period ended up being no more defensible than under the Howard government which preceded it and the Coalition governments which followed.

The only domestic human rights advance of any real note during the Abbott–Turnbull–Morrison governments was the recognition of same-sex marriage, which owed far more to community sentiment—reflected in the overwhelming support shown in the reluctantly initiated 2017 postal survey—than any government conviction. While some blows have been struck on behalf of unpalatable free speech on campuses and elsewhere— defensible in principle, but not always applauded on my side of politics—the record otherwise has been bleak. It includes resistance to a constitutional Voice for Indigenous Australians, continued draconian border-protection laws, overzealous restrictions against perceived foreign influence, foot-dragging on sexual misbehaviour issues, and overenthusiasm for the rights of religious organisations to discriminate against those not sharing their faith. Not to mention appointing as human rights commissioner a Liberal Party–affiliated conservative without even pretending to follow the transparent competitive process required by the UN Human Rights Council.

New issues do constantly arise, as with mandatory COVID-19 vaccination: whether my freedom not to be vaccinated stops (as I, for one, firmly believes it does) with your risk of being infected. They will go on being the subject of endless debate, usually with the battlelines wearyingly familiar—right versus left, conservatives versus radicals, interventionists versus libertarians. There have been many setbacks and frustrations along the way, differences continue on key issues, and many battles remain to be fought. But, while the record is mixed, and much of the advance has been driven more by culture change from below than leadership from above, it would be fair to conclude that the broad trend has been towards greater respect and tolerance for individual difference and choice. Recognition of same-sex marriage, much more evidently visceral community hostility to racism, and far more obvious sensitivity on gender-respect issues, are major Australian achievements in recent times. So, on the internal human rights dimension of good international citizenship, complete consensus remains elusive, but we are inching closer to where we ought to be when measured against the highest international standards.

Looking Outward

When it comes to the external dimension, Australia's record has also been mixed, but with the overall direction less clear. Even with those governments who have wanted to do the right thing internationally, have taken international human rights standards seriously, and have been willing to help negotiate and sign up to new normative treaties, uncertainty has often been expressed as to just how far Australia—or any country—should go in responding to serious human rights violations occurring inside another sovereign state. Our international behaviour, reflecting that uncertainty, has been erratic.

South African apartheid, for decades the most visibly indefensible breach anywhere of the racial equality provisions of the UN charters, was for far too long defended on the conservative side of Australian politics as no-one else's business, or a matter of concern only to communist sympathisers. It took Malcolm Fraser, always admirable on race issues, to force a change of Coalition direction, and under Bob Hawke Australia played an important leadership role—particularly in our global advocacy of the case for financial sanctions, not just trade, sport and cultural boycotts—in the international campaign to bring down the apartheid regime. We have also played a leading global role, as will be discussed in the next section, in giving voice to the wider international community's responsibility to protect peoples at risk of genocide and other mass atrocity crimes, of the kind that occurred so horrifically in Cambodia, Rwanda and Bosnia.

But successive governments have not been very consistent on these issues. There is a deep reluctance on both sides of politics, for example, to call out as a new form of apartheid Israel's indefensibly discriminatory behaviour towards Palestinians in the Occupied Territories. And fears are routinely expressed by government policymakers and those who advise them that expressing human rights concerns, particularly if the misbehaving state is a significant economic or military player, will prejudice economic relations or create new security problems.

The possibility of upsetting friends or neighbours causes particular anxiety.

My strong personal view is that most of these anxieties are misplaced. In my long experience as foreign minister of making démarches to unsympathetic governments, I found that such fears are almost invariably overblown. Australia was a persistent advocate around the world throughout my term on issues like prisoners of conscience, executions, free speech, participatory democracy, and discrimination and violence against minorities. While I can remember causing a fair degree of discomfort, and on occasion irritation, with some of these representations, this was never to the point of having any subsequent adverse impact on Australia's economic or security interests. I took the view that if international attention made governments who behave badly feel even just a little discomfited, that was a consummation devoutly to be wished.

There is very little downside risk provided certain principles are observed. Be absolutely consistent from country to country in making your approaches: your credibility will not amount to much if you adjust your messages according to the trade balances involved or whether the authoritarianism in issue is of a right- or left-wing variety. Always emphasise the universality of the rights in question, avoiding any hint that you are in the business of exporting your own country's or 'Western' values. Respect the ground rules of neighbourhood civility and avoid overdoing Australian-style directness in face-to-face communication. And, so far as possible, make any such representations within a larger context of dialogue and engagement, so human rights and democracy do not come across as single-issue obsessions.

Applying this kind of approach, I was able to persuade my Chinese counterpart Qian Qichen in 1991, just two years after the Tiananmen massacre, to accept a ten-day visit from an Australian 'Human Rights Delegation' of parliamentarians, human rights experts and China scholars. Although they proved to be possibly the most inquisitive single group of foreigners to arrive on Chinese soil since Marco Polo, no harm was done and maybe a little good. And a precedent was established for much more substantial and regular intergovernmental dialogue on these issues for many subsequent years. Things have since changed with China, and I do not suggest that, under the present authoritarian and assertive leadership of Xi Jinping, any such progress could now be made. But although 'incessant wanton interference in China's Xinjiang, Hong Kong [and Taiwan] affairs' features among China's November 2020 list of fourteen grievances against Australia, I do not believe that our voicing of human rights objections has significantly contributed, by itself, to our currently fraught bilateral relations. Beijing knows that some such criticism comes with the territory in its relations with many Western countries, albeit not a lot of others.

Of course, the question has to be addressed as to how much practical difference any of this activity really does make, and what, in all the circumstances, are the most sensible things to do if one wants to effectively promote human rights values. My golden rule in this respect, and I believe this is what good international citizenship entails in this context, has always been this: *Do that which is productive; minimise, but don't entirely exclude, doing that which is unproductive; and avoid at all costs doing that which is counterproductive.*

Sometimes the actions that our governments take, both bilaterally and in multilateral forums, in responding to human rights violations in other countries, are manifestly unproductive. But that does not mean they should not be engaged in at all, if only on a modest scale. I took that view as foreign minister in regularly instructing my often rather unhappy diplomats to make representations to their host country counterparts in relation to Amnesty International–supplied advice about imminent executions or particular political prisoners. We had no obvious impact in other than a tiny handful of the hundreds of cases raised (in 1993 alone, 534 new cases in ninety countries).[19] But these representations did make clear—I think usefully—that at least someone in the wider international community was watching and monitoring these countries' behaviour.

What clearly has to be avoided by governments, however enthusiastically they might want to demonstrate their good international citizenship credentials, is human rights activity that is manifestly counterproductive for the people sought to be helped. Although the preference that many governments express for 'quiet diplomacy' on these matters tends to infuriate NGOs, this is not always a cynical cover for not making any waves at all. It can sometimes be the only sensible way to proceed, because noisy diplomacy can seriously stiffen resistance, with national leaders not wanting to be seen to be yielding to visible international pressure. One recent example may have been Indonesian President Jokowi's determination, in the face of a strong and very public Australian campaign in 2015, to proceed with the execution of the convicted drug offenders Andrew Chan and Myuran Sukumaran.

A case that will live long in my memory is how close we came in 1994 to a major autonomy package for the brutally suppressed people of East Timor. After years of quietly working with my Indonesian foreign minister counterpart Ali Alatas to achieve this, it was on the verge of being announced by president Soeharto at that year's Asia-Pacific Economic Cooperation (APEC) meeting—until a well-intentioned statement from president Bill Clinton in Jakarta, designed to pressure Soeharto into accepting such a package, produced, as this kind of diplomacy sometimes does, precisely the opposite result.

Being a good international citizen, here as elsewhere, certainly means being committed to doing the right thing morally. But that does not mean being oblivious to real-world constraints. A recurring theme of this essay is that, sometimes, the best really is the enemy of the good.

AUSTRALIA'S RECORD: CONFLICT, ATROCITIES AND REFUGEES

The third benchmark by which a country's standing as a good international citizen should be assessed is whether it is doing everything it reasonably can to achieve international peace and security; to prevent or respond to the horror and misery of war and mass atrocity crimes; and to alleviate their consequences, including for those fleeing their impact.

A country of Australia's middle-power status, lacking the kind of diplomatic clout that comes with permanent membership of the UN Security Council, or the degree of military or economic power that is inherently capable of bending other countries to its will, can never, even at the best of times, expect to be a decisive player on matters of peace and war, or in preventing or halting mass atrocity crimes. And in the present deteriorating global and regional security environment, the opportunities for effective engagement are even fewer. But when it comes to alleviating the human distress that so often comes in the aftermath of deadly conflict—in particular that of refugees and asylum seekers—we have as much responsibility, and capacity, as any other country in the world.

Whatever the actual power we have in these different contexts, we always have a choice as to whether to be a responsible or an irresponsible player. And Australia has in the past been both. In peacemaking diplomacy, and responding to mass atrocity crimes, we have played some important positive roles, notably in Cambodia. As international peacekeepers we have always done well, but accepted too few such obligations in recent years. In the case of actual warfighting we have been at our best when making our own decision to fight just wars, in accordance with the legal principles now embodied in the UN Charter, and at our worst when persuaded to go to war for less than just causes in the hope that by doing so we will buy alliance insurance protection against possible future threats to ourselves. When it comes to meeting our responsibilities to refugees and asylum seekers, our good international citizenship record is again very mixed: at times in the past a very proud one, but in recent years little short of shameful.

Peacemaking

When the United Nations was created in 1945, Australia's Dr HV Evatt is universally acknowledged to have played a hugely creative role in developing its collective security architecture. In the fraught Cold War decades that followed there were few, if any, opportunities for a country of our size and weight to contribute diplomatically to global or regional peace and security, either in institution building or in response to particular conflict situations. But things changed in the early post–Cold War years. US–Soviet tensions had evaporated, US–China strains were still years away, and the UN Security Council was cooperatively inclined. The late 1980s and early 1990s was a period when almost anything seemed possible—one when, as I put it in my (now rather implausibly titled) 2017 memoir *Incorrigible Optimist*, 'Bliss was it in that dawn to be alive, but to be Foreign Minister was very heaven!' And it was an opportunity of which the Hawke government took full advantage.

We played a central role in developing new multilateral dialogue institutions in the region—the APEC forum at leadership level (economics focused, but providing the opportunity for major security discussions in the margins), and the ASEAN Regional Forum (ARF) at ministerial level (an institution with great potential, albeit not fully realised subsequently, for cooperative conflict prevention and resolution). We contributed well-received new thinking about the UN's potential role in peacemaking, peacekeeping, peace enforcement and peacebuilding in the 250-page 'blue book' launched at the General Assembly in 1993.[20] We generated new thinking about nuclear disarmament by initiating the Canberra Commission described in the next section. We played a central, and widely heralded, role in bringing the Convention on the Prohibition of Chemical Weapons to conclusion.

Perhaps most importantly of all, Australia was the driving force behind the process which brought peace to Cambodia, a country terribly ravaged by US Vietnam War bombing, the Khmer Rouge's genocidal reign of terror, and ongoing civil war. With irreconcilable internal divisions, South-East Asia fractured, and Russia, China and the United States all taking different sides, this was the region's most intractable conflict. Bill Hayden first tilled the soil, particularly with Vietnam, which I was able to fully cultivate when I succeeded him as foreign minister. The circuit-breaker we came up with was the proposal for the UN to play an unprecedentedly central role in administering the country during a transitional period, thereby giving China a face-saving way to withdraw its support for the Khmer Rouge. Developed in close cooperation with Indonesia, this proved the breakthrough which led to the Paris Peace Conference in 1991, UN-supervised elections in 1993, a final end to all hostilities, and the normalisation of diplomatic relationships around the region. Thirty years on, that peace still holds—even if the democracy and human rights transformation we also hoped for remains, sadly, very much unfinished business—and Australia is still credited as the prime mover in achieving it.[21]

It is hard to point to any similarly successful diplomatic initiatives in subsequent years, although successive governments have contributed to the establishment and development since 2005 of the East Asian Summit, which is potentially—though not yet actually—the region's most important leadership-level dialogue institution. And the Coalition, inheriting a UN Security Council seat in 2013–14—after opposing Labor's campaign for it following a 27-year absence—did play a generally active and constructive role there on global security issues, especially in leading the charge for humanitarian access to Syria. The reality is that the re-emergence and intensification of great-power rivalry over the last two decades has again made effective international action in the prevention and resolution of conflict, with a role for countries like Australia, very difficult to achieve—even for governments much more instinctively enthusiastic about playing that role than Coalition governments in Australia have traditionally been.

Peacekeeping

This is an area where Australia has consistently enhanced its reputation, even if it is the case that the small scale of many of our individual commitments, and their reduced overall level over the last two decades, has not fully matched our capacity. Australia had its first such operation, which most often have been conducted under UN authority, as part of a military observation mission in 1947. Our most intense levels of UN engagement were in the 1990s, in particular with the United Nations Transitional Authority in Cambodia (UNTAC, outstandingly commanded by our general John Sanderson) and the United Nations Operation in Somalia (UNOSOM), with at one stage in 1993 over 2000 military and police peacekeepers in the field in these two missions alone. Other high-profile operations have been the Australian-led International Force East Timor (Interfet) in 1999–2000, involving 5500 personnel as a non-UN force but acting in accordance with UN resolutions, and the successful Regional Assistance Mission to the Solomon Islands (RAMSI) from 2003 to 2013, acting in response to a request from our neighbour, over the course of which more than 7000 Australian personnel were deployed.[22]

Over time the concept, and practice, of peacekeeping has dramatically evolved—from relatively straightforward ceasefire monitoring to much more comprehensive stabilisation and peacebuilding operations. But what has not changed over the years is the very high regard in which Australian peacekeepers are held internationally, both among fellow professionals and in the local communities in which they have served. I can confirm this from my own direct observations both as foreign minister and then later, for nearly a decade, as head of the International Crisis

Group. There does seem to be something instinctively egalitarian about Australians, whatever their background, education or life experience. There is an absolute willingness to take others as they find them, neither sucking up nor kicking down; responding to the way others behave, not the way they look, or dress or talk; and whatever their station in life. Of course there will always be exceptions, but this culture does seem to overwhelmingly prevail when Australians are serving in community environments abroad—at least in peacekeeping and peacebuilding, if not always warfighting, situations.

Everything just said is also applicable to those thousands of Australians who have acted as 'humanitarian peacekeepers' in combined civilian and military offshore emergency relief operations. These began with our medical response to the impact of the Spanish flu in the South Pacific in 1918, were followed by responses to volcano eruptions in Papua New Guinea in 1937 and 1951, and then took off on a regular basis after 1960, with dozens of significant interventions since then around the Pacific and South-East Asia, and occasionally further afield, not least in the harrowing Aceh disaster relief operation after the catastrophic 2004 tsunami.[23]

Peacekeeping and humanitarian relief operations are good international citizenship at its finest. It is just a pity that Australia's more recent global peacekeeping contributions (in 2021, just four deployments in the Middle East and Africa, with a combined total of sixty personnel)[24] have been much smaller than our wealth makes possible, and that our sense of global responsibility should demand.

Warfighting

Good international citizens do not have to be pacifists. But when it comes to full-scale warfighting, they should not initiate or participate in military action unless the use of force is clearly justified under international law, or morally, or preferably both. And Australia has not always observed these constraints.

The legal grounds for the permissible use of military force are clear enough under the UN Charter: only in self-defence (Article 51), or if authorised by the Security Council in response to 'any threat to the peace, breach of the peace or act of aggression' (Chapter VII, with a little leeway for action by UN-recognised regional organisations under Chapter VIII). When it is *morally* right to fight—and whether warfighting can be legal but not legitimate, or legitimate but not legal—will, in the absence of any comparably authoritative international ruling, always be subject to argument. But intense debate around the issue over the last two decades—stimulated initially by NATO's Kosovo intervention, which had been vetoed in the Security Council but was very widely seen as morally defensible—has produced what I would argue to be a broad consensus around five basic criteria of legitimacy. These are very familiar from traditional Christian 'just war' doctrine but also resonate in religious and cultural traditions right around the world. In short, they are the *seriousness of the threat*; whether the *primary purpose* of the proposed military action is to halt or avert that threat; whether force is a *last resort*, with reasonable grounds for believing lesser measures would not succeed; whether the scale, duration and intensity of the action is *proportional* to the threat; and, perhaps most important of all, the *balance of consequences*—whether the military action will do more good than harm.[25]

Australia has not always observed these constraints. No-one seriously argues about either the legality or moral legitimacy of our fighting in World War II against Nazi Germany and Japan; or in the 1950–53 Korean War under the UN flag; or in the first Gulf War of 1991 following Iraq's invasion of Kuwait, which was condemned by the UN Security Council; or—though our motivation was less obviously high-minded—our joining at least the early stages of the UN-supported post-9/11 operation against Afghanistan, or the campaign against the Islamic State jihadists in Syria and Iraq since 2014. But the hugely destructive US-led war against North Vietnam from 1965 to 1973 was an utterly misconceived enterprise from start to finish—misreading nationalism as messianic communist expansionism—in which Australia should have played no part. And that against Iraq in 2003 was even more comprehensively indefensible, in the absence of any credible rationale in terms of the possession of weapons of mass destruction, or terrorist activity, or—at least at that time, whatever may have been the case years earlier—massive human rights violations.

We went to war in Vietnam and Iraq, and stayed in Afghanistan much longer than we should have, not because these fights were justified in law or morality, but because the United States wanted us to, or we thought they wanted us to, or because we wanted them to want us to. Successive governments have believed, or wanted to believe, that in doing so they were buying insurance for our future defence should we ourselves ever be at serious risk. But it is naïve to believe that all these down-payments in blood, let alone a 'century of mateship', mean that the United States will be there for us militarily in any circumstance where it does not also see its own immediate interests being under threat. The ANZUS Treaty requires the United States 'to act' should we come under attack, but does not require that action to be military. The reality of US self-interest and self-absorption has been clear enough for those with eyes to see under previous administrations, but was thrown into much starker relief by Trump's 'America First' approach, and most recently by the debacle of the 2021 withdrawal from Afghanistan. Anyone who believes that Washington's focus will ever be more than primarily inward-looking, even under a manifestly more civilised administration (which certainly cannot be guaranteed in the future), simply has not been concentrating.

This concern has underlain a good deal of the anxiety generated by Australia's AUKUS agreement in September 2021 to partner with the US and UK in massive new defence technology acquisitions, with eight or more nuclear-powered submarines the centrepiece. The deal is on balance defensible, with a number of other concerns, including its potential contribution to nuclear weapons proliferation, being overhyped, as I have discussed in detail elsewhere.[26] But there is a real issue as to whether Australia will become so much more enmeshed operationally with the United States that it will be impossible for us to resist demands that we join it in yet more wars in which it would not be at all in our own interests to engage. That concern will only be allayed if our political leaders in the decades ahead are unwavering in holding the Americans to their clear assurances that there will be 'no follow-on reciprocal requirements of any kind' and 'no quid pro quo'. We win no respect or credibility anywhere by being cast as anyone's 'deputy sheriff'.

The bottom line is *not* that we should never go to war other than in our own self-defence. Being, and being seen to be, a good international citizen may require a little more than that. There will be occasions when not only is the legal justification clear, but the moral obligation is compelling, and we have the resources available to help make a difference, with other allies or partners. Such occasions may involve states waging aggressive war against helpless neighbours. Or they may involve them perpetrating, or allowing to be perpetrated, genocide or other mass atrocity crimes against their own citizens.

Atrocities

Even after the horrors of the Holocaust, and the adoption in 1948 of the UN Convention on the Prevention and Punishment of Genocide, genocide, ethnic cleansing, other crimes against humanity and large-scale war crimes—the worst human rights violations of all—remained in subsequent decades a shamefully recurring reality. Cambodia in the 1970s, with the Khmer Rouge responsible for up to two million deaths, was thought to be as bad as things could get, until the catastrophes in Rwanda and the Balkans brought the issue explosively back to life in the 1990s. But when it came to effective reaction, the international community was, until twenty years ago, a consensus-free zone. The global North talked up, but rarely acted on, 'humanitarian intervention' or 'the right to intervene' militarily, while the global South, having long suffered imperial *missions civilisatrices*, rejected any such 'right' to breach their recently hard-won sovereignty.

It was not until 2001, with the publication of *The Responsibility to Protect* by the International Commission on Intervention and State Sovereignty (ICISS), that the impasse was broken. The ICISS report, by proposing that the focus be on 'responsibility' rather than 'right', and 'protection' rather than 'intervention', changed the whole language of the debate. And, by focusing on prevention and other forms of reaction, like targeted sanctions and criminal prosecution, rather than military action (although not excluding it as a last resort, if the UN Security Council agreed), it shifted the whole substance of the debate. There was a new set of proposed prohibitions—challenging sovereign immunity though they did—on which the global South could now agree. And they did. Their support for 'the responsibility to protect' (now universally abbreviated as 'R2P') ensured its unanimous adoption by the UN General Assembly at the 2005 World Summit, and subsequently by the Security Council.[27]

Australia and Australians have played a significant part in this whole enterprise. I was privileged to be asked by Canada to co-chair ICISS and, with my Australian colleague Ramesh Thakur—along with Canada's Michael Ignatieff—drafted its report. Australian diplomats, led by our then UN ambassador John Dauth, played a central role in getting it endorsed by the whole global community. Successive Australian governments, both Coalition and Labor, have been strong supporters of its practical application, actively participating at foreign minister level in 'Friends of R2P' advocacy in New York and Geneva, and giving generous financial support to the non-governmental, New York–based Global Centre for the Responsibility to Protect—the key global research and advocacy organisation, long headed by Australia's Simon Adams—and its influential regional counterpart, the Asia-Pacific Centre for R2P, based in Brisbane and headed by Queensland University's Alex Bellamy.

Plenty of cynics can be heard saying none of this has really made any difference. And looking at the mass atrocities that have continued to occur in places like Sri Lanka, Myanmar, Yemen and above all Syria, not to mention China's persecution of its Uyghurs, they have an obvious point. But for all that continues to go wrong, real progress has been made. *Normatively*, as evidenced in annual General Assembly debates and multiple Security Council resolutions, R2P has achieved global acceptance— unimaginable for 'humanitarian intervention'—as a new standard of international behaviour which, overwhelmingly if not universally, states feel ashamed to violate, compelled to observe, or at least embarrassed to ignore. *Institutionally*, real progress has been made in developing both international legal accountability mechanisms, and national civilian and military response preparedness. *Preventively*, R2P-driven strategies have had a number of successes, notably in stopping the recurrence of violence in Kenya, in the West African cases of Sierra Leone, Liberia, Guinea, Côte d'Ivoire and The Gambia, and in Kyrgyzstan, while volatile situations such as Burundi get Security Council attention of a kind unknown to Rwanda in the 1990s. But as so often is the case with effective prevention, when nothing bad actually happens, nobody notices.

Reactively—ensuring an effective response to atrocity crises actually underway—R2P is obviously still a work in progress. There have been partial successes—more often involving diplomatic rather than military pressure—in Kenya, Côte d'Ivoire, Congo, South Sudan, and the Central African Republic, and even Libya (at least initially, in stopping a massacre in Benghazi). But also too many failures, not helped by the re-emergence of major-power rivalry and obstruction in the Security Council. That said, as Kofi Annan put it so graphically in his 2000 *Millennium Report*—so inspirational to me and everyone else working for R2P—these cases 'are gross and systematic violations of human rights that offend every precept of our common humanity'. Ending mass atrocity crimes once and for all—ensuring that 'Never Again' actually means something—is not a cause on which any country which values its good international credentials can ever give up, and I hope and expect that Australia will not.

Refugees

The compassion and generosity with which a country treats refugees—or asylum seekers, in the case of those whose status is not yet resolved—is as clear a test of good international citizenship as there could be. Australia has been a party almost from the outset to both the 1951 Europe-focused Convention on the Status of Refugees, and the 1967 Protocol extending its scope worldwide, and proudly claims to have resettled 920 000 refugees and others in need since World War II.[28] But our record has only rarely been as good as it could have been.[29] And in recent years—in a world the UN High Commissioner for Refugees now estimates to have some thirty million refugees and asylum seekers fleeing persecution, conflict and human rights abuses, most of them now languishing in neighbouring developing countries—that record has been lamentable.

Until the 1970s our refugee intake, though reasonably generous, at some 10 000 a year, given the size of our then population, was buried in the larger immigration program and tarnished by its racial selectivity, wholly governed by the White Australia policy. The Whitlam government abolished racial selectivity but accepted only a handful of those fleeing Vietnam and Cambodia, anxious about their likely strongly anti-left political sympathies. The biggest stride forward was made by Malcolm Fraser—having no such political inhibitions but also, as always, genuinely colour-blind—whose government resettled tens of thousands of Vietnamese refugees, including 'boat people': more per capita than any other country. That policy was continued by the Hawke government, with the result that between 1975 and 1991 Australia had resettled over 130 000 Indochinese refugees.[30] And Bob Hawke famously reacted to the Tiananmen massacre in 1989 by offering temporary residence to Chinese nationals then in Australia, with 42 000 eventually being granted permanent visas.

Under Paul Keating as prime minister from late 1991 to 1996, humanitarian arrivals averaged 12 000 a year—again among the highest in the world on a per-capita basis—but the domestic political environment was becoming more difficult, with the Liberal Party having become much less liberal under Howard's leadership. The arrival of a few 'boat people' from Cambodia triggered the introduction in 1992 of mandatory detention for all unauthorised arrivals—in retrospect, a major shift presaging the rot which was to follow, in terms of a steady diminution in the decency with which both asylum seekers and refugees were treated. Under Howard's own government, from 1996 to 2007 the trickle of draconian measures, all of them either indefensible or problematic under international refugee law, became a flood. Administrative and judicial review was restricted; successful applicants for refugee status were granted only temporary, not permanent, protection and denied any right to sponsor spouses or children, or to re-enter Australia if they left for any reason, however compassionate; and, in the aftermath of the *Tampa* affair, offshore processing—the 'Pacific solution'—was introduced for all unauthorised arrivals.

The *Tampa* affair in August 2001, when the government denied permission to a Norwegian container ship to disembark 433 mostly Afghan asylum seekers whom it had rescued from their sinking vessel at Australian request, was particularly catastrophic for Australia's international reputation, But Howard continued to demonise all 'boat people', much more concerned with playing to domestic populist sentiment, as he was with the 9/11 attacks, stoking fears of potential terrorists sneaking entry, and with a national election imminent. This reached its most shameless depth in October 2001, when the government claimed, completely falsely, that the occupants of a boat being turned back from Australian waters (another post-*Tampa* policy) had thrown their children overboard to force the navy to rescue them, and continued to insist this even after being corrected by its own military.

Labor's opposition to the Howard policy was anything but robust, but when Kevin Rudd became prime minister in 2007, a major, if short-lived, effort was made to change course. Temporary protection visas were abolished, the Nauru and Manus Island 'Pacific solution' centres closed, and mandatory detention of unauthorised arrivals was limited, but with those coming by sea still sent to Christmas Island. And Julia Gillard, who replaced Rudd in 2010, significantly increased the overall size of the refugee and humanitarian program. But as sea arrivals began to surge, and Coalition 'Stop the boats' attacks under Tony Abbott as Opposition leader became relentless, Labor wilted. Most of the Howard-era policies were successively reinstated, with Gillard reopening the Nauru and Manus centres, and Rudd—during his brief return in 2013—announcing that successful applicants for refugee status would be settled in Papua New Guinea, Nauru or a third country, but not Australia. A creative and wholly laudatory attempt was made by the Gillard government to avoid re-embracing the 'Pacific solution', by sending asylum seekers to Malaysia for processing in exchange for a much larger number of approved refugees. But the 'Malaysian solution' was eventually defeated in the Senate when the Greens joined forces with the Coalition, not because the proposal was bad, but because it was not good enough—repeating exactly the kind of unforgivable misjudgement they had shown earlier in opposing Rudd's Carbon Pollution Reduction Scheme (CPRS), on which more below.

The Abbott–Turnbull–Morrison Coalition governments since 2013 have done nothing but further tarnish Australia's good international citizenship standing in this space, with about the only positive note being Abbott's agreement in 2015 to accept 12 000 Syrians fleeing their country's civil war, a response not even begun to be matched by the Morrison government for Afghans in their hour of need in 2021. A case can be mounted in defence of a continued strong policy of naval turnbacks of unauthorised boat arrivals—people-smugglers do have to be deterred from resuming their ugly trade, with the deaths at sea that inevitably accompany it. But it is highly questionable whether offshore processing has been an indispensable additional contribution to that deterrent. And there can be no defence at all of the appalling inhumanity with which asylum seekers have for so long been treated when it comes to conditions in the detention centres, and their medical and human needs (the harrowing experience of Behrouz Boochani on Manus and the Murugappan family from Biloela being among the best known and documented).[31] Nor of the unwillingness to allow so many actually determined to be refugees to resettle in Australia, and the shamelessness of some of the efforts—above all with Cambodia—to buy options elsewhere. Nor of the miserliness of our annual refugee and humanitarian overall intakes—less than 14 000 for 2021–22—given the current numbers globally of those displaced, which are likely to grow greater still with those now wanting to flee Afghanistan with the Taliban regaining power.

One of the most extraordinary features of the whole 'boat people' debate in Australia over the last two decades is how often it has been conducted on an almost entirely emotional, rather than rational, basis. The current extreme 'no blinking' Fortress Australia approach of the Morrison government ignores the fact that multiple blinks in the past—for example, Howard's initial settlement in Australia of Manus and Nauru detainees—have not resulted in new armadas. Turnbacks have been sufficient disincentive. Perhaps when combined with offshore processing, but there is strong evidence that the latter has added nothing to deterrence.[32] It seems to be constantly ignored, or forgotten, that while almost countless measures have been adopted to stop boat arrivals, and make life utterly miserable for those who do manage to get through, there have been many thousands of arrivals by air, usually with tourist visas, who have subsequently overstayed, claimed refugee status and been unsuccessful, but who are still living in the community—27 000 at last count.[33] What is it about boats, and not planes, that makes political leaders incapable of any kind of principled, rational leadership?

While both sides of politics have been engaged in a populist race to the bottom on asylum seekers for too many years, perhaps the nadir was reached with our response in May 2015 to the plight of 7000 Rohingya and Bangladeshis stranded at sea, when Malaysia and Indonesia said they would allow them ashore on condition they could be repatriated or resettled within a year. Asked whether Australia could help with that resettlement, then prime minister Abbott's reply was 'Nope, nope, nope'. Which neatly combined—in three words, inevitably—both a perception of distaste for multilateral problem-solving, and a profound indifference to our common humanity.

AUSTRALIA'S RECORD: PANDEMICS, CLIMATE AND NUCLEAR WEAPONS

The fourth, and final, benchmark helpful in determining whether a country deserves the status of a good international citizen is whether it is an actively committed participant in collaborative and cooperative attempts to solve the biggest of all collective-action problems: the great existential risks posed by health pandemics, global warming and nuclear war.

Good international citizenship, as I have described it, requires almost by definition a cooperative mindset. That includes, in particular, being willing to engage in collective international action to advance those regional and global public goods problems which are by their nature beyond the capacity of any one state, however powerful, to solve individually. By far the most pressing of these 'problems without passports' are the three posing a real threat not just to particular populations, countries or regions, but to life on this planet as we know it. The COVID crisis has been a huge wake-up call in relation to health pandemics. On climate change, the ranks of the doubtful on its nature and impact—even within Australia's conservative government—are rapidly diminishing. But on nuclear weapons, there is still an alarming degree of complacency, among both publics and policymakers, when it comes to the risks of nuclear war.

On all three of these fronts, Australia's international performance has been underwhelming or worse, ranging from a bare pass in the case of pandemics to a dismal fail on climate change. On nuclear weapons, the verdict is more nuanced. Australia has played a useful role in the past, and can again in the future, on nuclear risk reduction, and ultimate elimination. But in recent years our contribution has been more of an encumbrance than an encouragement. On both climate and nuclear arms control in particular, we have a real responsibility, both in moral and national interest terms, to do better, and there is much that we have not been doing that we can.

Pandemics

No issue in memory has cried out more for international cooperation and compassion than the COVID-19 pandemic since it spread from China throughout the rest of the world in 2020. By the time of this writing, in late 2021, there have been nearly five million documented deaths worldwide, with mortality in many countries likely to have been seriously under-reported. A stark gulf has certainly become apparent between high- and low-income countries when it comes to vaccine rollout, with the World Health Organization reporting in August 2021 that less than 20 per cent of the doses administered had gone to low- and lower-middle-income countries, and that while high-income countries have on average administered 100 doses for each 100 people, low-income countries have only managed 1.5. It is not easy to justify rich countries hoarding vaccines for discretionary third-round booster shots when hundreds of millions around the world are still waiting for their first.[34]

A troubling dimension of the crisis—and one from which Australia has not been immune—has been its impact in turning both policymakers and publics much more visibly inward: demanding border closures and tough immigration controls, being fearful about foreigners and 'the other', and being much readier to employ the language of sovereignty, nationalism and self-protection. Good international citizenship is not an easy sell in this environment. But while it is both unsurprising, and perfectly defensible, to be preoccupied with one's own country's sick and dying more than anyone else's, there are not only moral but practical national interest reasons— not least in consolidating a reputation for being a decent country—for setting limits to self-absorption.

In the international response to COVID, Australia cannot realistically be expected to be more than a bit player. Our one big effort to become more than that, trying in 2020 to lead the charge to establish an international inquiry into the Chinese origins of COVID-19, was a counterproductive mess: ill-thought-out operationally, underprepared diplomatically, having no impact institutionally on the terms of the final WHO resolution, and serving only to make our already fragile bilateral relationship with China a good deal worse. But we do have a voice in multiple relevant international organisations, and should use it responsibly. It is not always clear that we have. While we have always strongly supported the WHO, we have dragged our feet there in backing a waiver of patents and other intellectual property rights on vaccines, diagnostic tests and devices needed to fight the current pandemic. And this in an environment where COVAX—the global program for distributing vaccines equitably—has fallen massively short of its intended target of two billion doses by the end of 2021.[35]

Nor is it clear that, despite our announced commitment to making vaccines available to our neighbours in the South Pacific through our aid program, Australia has been as responsive or generous as we could be. With PNG in particular in real crisis, by October 2021 we had delivered just 8 per cent of our promised donations to the region. Nor have we shown any commitment to the long haul, announcing that supply contracts with manufacturers will not be renewed once the donation target of fifty million doses has been met. And our financial contribution to COVAX has been among the least generous of any developed country.[36]

Against all this, Australia ranks well in one measure of helping others: the ratio of COVID doses pledged abroad to those delivered at home. And we do have world-ranking immunology research institutions like the Walter and Eliza Hall and Doherty institutes, world-class epidemiologists like the ANU's Professor Kamalini Lokuge, and a world-class vaccine producer in CSL, all of whom have played their part both in past pandemics and the current crisis. Overall, internationally, we can be given a pass, but only a very bare one.

Climate

It's a different story with respect to climate change. If there was ever any remaining room for doubt about the scale of the existential risk to the planet posed by global warming, it was comprehensively dispelled by the sixth report of the Intergovernmental Panel on Climate Change (IPCC), published in August 2021, warning that a global temperature rise of 1.5 degrees Celsius above pre-industrial levels—along with the multiple extreme weather events that come with it—is now virtually inevitable, and that the longer-term goal of keeping warming below 2 degrees is now profoundly at risk. Climate change is not coming, it has arrived. Its causes are 'unequivocally' human; and its implications, not least for Australia, are alarming. Achieving deep carbon cuts in the next ten years will be absolutely critical in holding any kind of line.

UN Secretary-General António Guterres described the report as 'code red for humanity'.

Unlike our capacity to make a major international contribution on pandemics, Australia is, and is seen to be, anything but a bit player on climate. We are a huge player in global energy markets: the largest exporter in the world of liquefied natural gas, the second-largest exporter of thermal coal, and overall the third-largest fossil fuel exporter, behind only Saudi Arabia and Russia. We may, with our small population, contribute only around 1.3 per cent to total domestic global greenhouse emissions, but that puts us among the top dozen polluters in per-capita terms. Beyond that, we are the twelfth- or thirteenth-largest economy in the world, a member of the G20 (who played a recognised central role in formulating its policy response to the global financial crisis), and have a long record of punching diplomatically—when we choose to—well above our weight on economic and security issues. What we say and do on global warming matters.

That reality seems to have been, for too many of our policymakers, a matter of profound indifference. The Morrison government's insouciant parliamentary response to the IPCC report gave further evidence, if any were needed, of the lamentable irresponsibility of far too much Australian policymaking on this subject. 'Nothing to see here' remained the storyline: the problem, if there is one, lies with other countries; there is no need to strengthen our 2015 Paris commitment of a 26–28 per cent reduction in emissions by 2030, even if most major economies are moving to almost double that number; there is no need to specifically commit to net-zero by 2050, even if that commitment is now becoming almost universal; there is no need for any price signals: 'technology, not taxes' will get us wherever we need to go. And Labor in Opposition, wrestling with its own internal policy struggle between inner-city and coal-seat warriors, showed little inclination on any of this to pin the Prime Minister to the wall.

That said, with a national election looming, public opinion moving overwhelmingly in favour of more decisive and effective action,[37] business leaders becoming much more outspoken about the need for decisive government leadership, and facing fierce international criticism at the COP26 Glasgow climate summit in November 2021, Australia at last adopted the current globally accepted target of net-zero emissions by 2050. But Morrison's announced 'plan' to get there has been legitimately attacked as embarrassingly substance-free.[38] And on the even more critical issue of strengthening the short-term 2030 target, his government, captive to the troglodyte majority of its National Party Coalition partner, has refused any further concession. Australia's position, at the time of writing in late 2021, is seen internationally as grudging, minimalist, and will do nothing to redeem our now well-established reputation as a climate laggard. It is extraordinary how much foot-dragging and backsliding there has been here, how often crude domestic and intra-party politics have prevailed over intelligent calculation of larger national interest, and how long it has taken here for even a semblance of good international citizenship to prevail.

Global environmental issues had nothing like the salience three decades ago that they have today. Bob Hawke, to his credit, saw the writing on the wall earlier and more clearly than most, above all with his initiation of the global campaign, culminating in the Madrid Protocol of 1991, to ban permanently mining and oil drilling in Antarctica. On climate-related threats, ozone layer depletion attracted public attention from the 1970s onward, and, because of the obviously urgent need to ban fluorocarbon release, resulted in effective early global action with the Montreal Protocol of 1987. There were plenty of early warnings—including in the mid-1980s from Australia's own very prescient Barry Jones—about the even larger, albeit longer-term, risks of global warming from the emission of 'greenhouse gases', carbon dioxide and methane in particular. But alarm bells really only started ringing in the 1990s, with the first reports of the IPCC, the signing of the UN Framework Convention on Climate Change at the 1992 Earth Summit, and the first attempts to set emissions targets, at least for developed countries, in the 1997 Kyoto Protocol.

In Australia, whatever emerging domestic consensus there had been in the early 1990s about the need for an effective policy response disappeared for more than a decade with the 1996 election. The new Howard Coalition government insisted that the scientific debate was not settled, argued that any international disciplines were meaningless unless applicable to developing as well as developed countries, and joined the United States as one of only two states refusing to ratify the Kyoto Protocol.

Prospects dramatically improved when the ALP won the 2007 election, with Kevin Rudd famously calling climate change the 'greatest moral, economic and social challenge of our time', immediately ratifying the Kyoto Protocol, and proposing, with the support of then Opposition leader Malcolm Turnbull, to give legislative substance to our commitment. But before any bill could be passed, Turnbull was deposed by the climate sceptic Tony Abbott, and Rudd's CPRS was defeated in the Senate, with the Greens making the catastrophically wrong-headed decision to join the Opposition in striking it down—not because it was too strong, but because it failed to meet their standards of perfection.

From there it was downhill all the way. Rudd lost his nerve and focus on the issue and, partly for that reason, was deposed in an internal party coup by Julia Gillard. After becoming impossibly tangled in contradictory statements about whether she did or did not oppose a carbon tax, she in turn was mortally wounded politically. Rudd's return did not stop Labor's defeat shortly thereafter in 2013 by the still rampantly climate denialist Tony Abbott. When Malcolm Turnbull deposed Abbott in 2015, in the continuing revolving-door circus of Australian politics of the period, hopes that he might steer Australia back to a more responsible position were soon confounded when it became clear that the price of his elevation was a commitment to the Coalition party room not to change its climate policy. Scott Morrison, who deposed him in turn in 2018, had, by contrast, no convictions on the subject which he needed to betray.

Australia has already paid a heavy reputational price internationally for this litany of failure. In June 2021, Jeffrey Sachs's UN-backed *Sustainable Development Report 2021* scored Australia *last* out of 193 UN member states for our performance on the 'climate action' goal. We received the lowest score awarded, just 10 out of 100, across the report's core metrics: the level of emissions from fossil fuel use, embedded emissions in imports and exports, and progress towards implementing an effective price on greenhouse gas emissions.[39] It has not escaped attention that, almost alone in the developed world, Australia's emissions from energy use actually *increased* between 2005 and the COVID pandemic. It is only by taking into account land clearing and logging, in accordance with the highly controversial 'Australia clause' on which we insisted in Kyoto, that we have been able to claim that our already very weak Paris commitment for 2030 is being met.[40]

The trouble has not stopped there. Our Prime Minister was denied, humiliatingly, a speaking slot at the UK-sponsored and strongly US-supported Climate Ambition Summit in December 2020, because of his refusal to commit Australia to strengthening our Paris emissions response. President Biden and his climate envoys have made clear their profound impatience with Australia's continued foot-dragging, although muting their public criticism in the context of the love-in associated with the AUKUS agreement discussed in the previous section. And we have lost friends and influence among our Pacific island neighbours, for most of whom a sea level rise is an immediate existential issue, and whose diplomatic leadership—which we completely undervalued—was crucial in achieving the 2015 Paris Agreement. In unprecedented snubs, they explicitly denied our request to join the High Ambition Coalition they initiated, and established a new Pacific Islands Development Forum to work around Australian obstruction in the traditional Pacific Islands Forum. All this at a time when larger geopolitical tensions with China have made our cooperative partnership with the region never more important.[41]

The irony is that Australia's determination to resist as long as possible the transformation of our fossil fuel economy, which has worked so much to our advantage in the past, will do us no favours in the future. It is only a matter of time before countries start taxing goods at the border based on the carbon emissions involved in producing them, as the US, EU and UK have already foreshadowed, in order to level the playing field between companies at home paying a carbon price and those abroad who are not. The larger point is that we have an abundance of renewable energy resources, and an enormous capacity to benefit economically from a clean energy revolution, as Ross Garnaut has shown in meticulous detail. He argues that, as the world's largest exporter of iron ore and alumina, and as a huge producer of other minerals, Australia 'in the post-carbon world' could become 'the locus of energy-intensive processing of minerals for use in countries with inferior renewable energy resource endowments'.[42] There could be few clearer examples than climate change that for Australia to behave as a good international citizen is not just a moral imperative but a national interest one.

Nuclear Weapons

Of the three great existential risks to life on this planet as we know it, the one about which both policymakers and publics, here and abroad, appear to be most complacent, is that flowing from nuclear war. On the face of it, that complacency is extraordinary. Nuclear weapons are not only the most indiscriminately inhumane ever devised, but the casualties that would follow any kind of significant nuclear exchange would be on an almost incalculably horrific scale. Not just from the immediate blast and longer-term radiation effects, but above all the catastrophic starvation-guaranteeing nuclear-winter effect on global agriculture.[43] And there is every prospect that, within the readily foreseeable future, those weapons will actually be used. The 'Doomsday Clock', published each year by the globally respected *Bulletin of the Atomic Scientists*, currently has its hands at 100 seconds to midnight, the closest they have been in the clock's long history.[44]

The risk starts with the still-massive size and trigger-readiness of the global nuclear arsenal. Despite the big reductions which occurred immediately after the end of the Cold War, and the continuing retirement or scheduling for dismantlement since by Russia and the United States of many more, over 13 000 warheads are still in existence, with a combined destructive capability of close to 100 000 Hiroshima- or Nagasaki-sized bombs. Around 6300 nuclear weapons remain in the hands of Russia, 5600 with the United States, and around 1300 with the other nuclear-armed states combined (China, France, the United Kingdom, India, Pakistan, Israel and—at the margin—North Korea). In our own Indo-Pacific region, delivery systems are being extended, weapons are being modernised and their numbers are increasing. A large proportion of the global stockpile—nearly 4000 weapons—remains operationally available. And, most extraordinarily of all, some 2000 of the US and Russian weapons remain on dangerously high alert, ready to be launched on warning in the event of a perceived attack, within a decision window for each president of four to eight minutes.[45]

These weapons may never be used coldly and deliberately to wage aggressive war. But there is a very high probability that they will, sooner or later, still be *used*. The fact that we have not had a nuclear weapon used in conflict for over seventy-five years is not a result of statesmanship, system integrity and infallibility, or the inherent stability of nuclear deterrence. It has been sheer dumb luck. Given what we now know about how many times the supposedly very sophisticated command-and-control systems of the Cold War years were strained by mistakes and false alarms, human error and human idiocy, given what we know about how much less sophisticated are the command-and-control systems of some of the newer nuclear-armed states, and given what we both know and can guess about how much more sophisticated and capable cyber-offence will be in overcoming cyber-defence in the years ahead, it is utterly wishful thinking to believe that this luck can continue in perpetuity.

The nuclear-armed states do acknowledge that there are risks associated with nuclear weapons. They talk constantly about the necessity of nuclear non-proliferation—the necessity to avoid the risks associated with new players joining the nuclear-armed club. And they talk constantly about the nuclear security risks associated with the acquisition of nuclear weapons or fissile material by rogue states or non-state terrorist actors. But they also constantly downplay the most immediate and real threat of them all: the risk of use by the present nuclear-armed states of their own existing arsenals—either with deliberately aggressive intent or, much more likely, as a result of accident or miscalculation, through system or human failure. And these are risks that can only be countered by the world's policymakers getting serious not just about nuclear non-proliferation and nuclear security, but nuclear *disarmament*.

It is this test that Australian Government policymakers, with only a handful of exceptions over the decades, have essentially failed. Successive governments have been actively committed supporters of non-proliferation through the Nuclear Non-Proliferation Treaty (NPT) and its associated International Atomic Energy Agency–administered safeguards system. We have outgrown our earlier accommodation of nuclear weapons testing by the United Kingdom on Australian soil, became very passionate when the French tested in our own Pacific neighbourhood, and strongly supported the Comprehensive Test Ban Treaty, with John Howard's government in fact playing a central role in bringing it to a conclusion in the UN General Assembly. We have supported the creation of Nuclear Weapon-Free Zones, and joined that in our own South Pacific region. We have been enthusiastic participants in the series of Nuclear Security Summits initiated by president Obama, aimed at ensuring that neither weapons nor nuclear fissile material ever get into the wrong hands. And we have made it abundantly clear that our proposed acquisition of nuclear-propelled submarines under the AUKUS agreement will be managed consistently with our non-proliferation responsibilities, and is in no way a prelude to Australia becoming nuclear-armed. But we have simply not been consistently serious about nuclear disarmament.

Various Labor governments have at least tried to move the dial. In 1996 prime minister Paul Keating and I initiated the Canberra Commission on the Elimination of Nuclear Weapons. With an all-star international cast, including from the United States Robert McNamara and the former strategic air commander general Lee Butler, this was the first international blue-ribbon panel to make a compelling case for the outright elimination of these weapons. Its central mantra—'So long as any state has nuclear weapons others will want them. So long as any state retains nuclear weapons they are bound one day to be used. And any such use will be catastrophic for life on this planet as we know it'—has been repeated by every high-level international panel since then which has addressed these issues. Including, in 2007, the jointly Australia–Japan sponsored International Commission on Nuclear Non-Proliferation and Disarmament initiated by

Kevin Rudd and co-chaired by me with former Japanese foreign minister Yoriko Kawaguchi, which not only made a strong case for an ultimate elimination agenda, but mapped a realistic 'minimisation' (or risk reduction) path to get there.[46]

But there has been no consistent follow-up to either of these initiatives, internationally well received though both were. Non-Labor governments have generally remained unhappily lovesick about nuclear deterrence, and the joys of sheltering uncritically under whatever nuclear umbrella the United States might be inclined to hold up for us in a crisis. Canberra has constantly taken its cue from Washington as to how far we can go. We have rarely added our voice to those arguing that the nuclear weapon states party to the NPT have a real obligation under that treaty to take serious steps toward disarmament. That has been notwithstanding the clear language of Article VI of the treaty, the reinforcing opinion of the International Court of Justice (in a case in which I represented Australia as foreign minister and former attorney-general to argue for illegality),[47] and this being seen by the non-weapon states as very much part of the bargain they entered into in foregoing any nuclear weapons ambitions of their own. It is very hard to avoid the label of hypocrisy when you take the position that your own security concerns justify nuclear weapons, but others' concerns do not.

Australia, again uncritically following the United States, has also refused to have anything to do with the Treaty on the Prohibition of Nuclear Weapons (TPNW). This treaty is a big normative step forward in delegitimising nuclear weapons, albeit binding only on those states joining it, which none of the nuclear-armed states are remotely likely to do. It was negotiated after a series of global 'humanitarian consequences' conferences in which Australia refused to even participate, and after a Nobel prize–winning effort by the International Campaign Against Nuclear Weapons (ICAN), an NGO founded here in Australia, whose achievement our Coalition government refused to even acknowledge, let alone congratulate. There are technical weaknesses in the TPNW treaty text (including the absence of any provisions for verification and, especially, enforcement), but the bigger problem has been a dogged belief by all the nuclear-armed states, and their allies and partners, in the continued utility of nuclear deterrence. There has been a total unwillingness to accept—as those hard-line Cold War realists Henry Kissinger, William Perry, Sam Nunn and the late George Shultz have done, in their famous series of *Wall Street Journal* articles since 2007—that in today's world the risks associated with nuclear weapons possession far outweigh any security returns.

In an environment where the achievement of 'Global Zero' remains manifestly out of reach for the indefinitely foreseeable future, it makes sense for those advocating a nuclear-weapon-free world not to make the best the enemy of the good. Rather, we should focus on nuclear risk reduction, finding common ground with those policymakers who may be uncomfortable abandoning what they still see as the ultimate deterrent and security guarantor, but nonetheless understand all the risks involved with nuclear weapons possession and want to minimise them.

The most commonly proposed risk-reduction measures—and central elements in our Australia–Japan commission's 'minimisation' agenda—may be described as the '4 Ds'. They are Doctrine (getting universal buy-in for a 'No First Use' commitment), Deployment (drastically reducing the number of weapons ready for immediate use), De-alerting (taking weapons off high-alert, launch-on warning readiness) and Decreased numbers (reducing the overall global stockpile to less than 2000 weapons). A world with low numbers of nuclear weapons, with very few of them physically deployed, with practically none of them on high-alert launch status, and with every nuclear-armed state visibly committed to never being the first to use them, would still be very far from perfect. But one that could achieve these objectives would be a very much safer world than we live in now.

What has been most depressing about Australia's performance in recent years is that even these realistic objectives have not been actively supported. Australia's status as a close US ally and, as such, one of the 'nuclear umbrella' states—together with our periodic high-profile international activism on arms-control issues—gives us a particularly significant potential role in advancing some key elements of the risk-reduction agenda just described. One especially important contribution would be to support the growing international movement for the universal adoption of 'No First Use' doctrine by the nuclear-armed states. President Obama was keen to go down the functionally equivalent path of a 'sole purpose' statement (namely, that nuclear weapons were held only to deter nuclear attack) but was dissuaded at the time by his North-East Asian, Central and Eastern European—and Australian—allies, all of whom wanted to cling tenaciously to an all-embracing nuclear security blanket. If another opportunity arises, as seems likely, with President Biden, there will hopefully be less timidity. That will need not only the election of a Labor government, but one that has recovered its mojo on these issues.

THE POLITICS OF DECENCY

Devotees of Charles Dickens will well remember that wonderfully philanthropically minded character in *Bleak House*, Mrs Jellyby, whose own large house is a riot of neglect—dirty and chaotic, filled with unwashed and badly dressed children, one of whom falls down the stairs completely unnoticed by her mother. She sits in the middle of it all with a faraway look in her eyes, focused on and consumed by nothing else than the needs of the poor, benighted denizens of Borrioboola-Gha in the heart of darkest Africa. For Dickens, driving the point home with his usual sledgehammer, *charity begins at home.*

That sentiment has long been entrenched in Australia's political psyche, influencing a great many policy choices. As mentioned earlier in this essay, I certainly have vivid memories of the battles I fought while foreign minister at budget time each year with finance minister Peter Walsh and the Expenditure Review Committee to keep my overseas aid program intact. They were the bloodiest I ever had to fight in Cabinet. Cutting development assistance was always seen as the easiest of all savings to make because few if any people at home would be affected, and there were always multiple competing domestic welfare needs to be met. For my colleagues, like Mr Dickens, charity did indeed begin at home. And, as described earlier, my predecessors and successors have all had the same problem.

What needs to be explored, however, is whether the sentiment in question is as equally firmly embedded in the mind of ordinary Australians as most politicians seem to think. The short answer, on all available evidence, is that it is not. If Australia has acted as a good international citizen much less consistently than it could have done, the problem—here, as indeed in other countries—lies not with the negative attitudes of our people, but with those of governments which have misread them.

Among the most recent of the many opinion surveys making this clear is the September 2020 Pew Research Center global survey of over 14 000 people across fourteen countries, including Australia, which found huge majority (81 per cent) support for the proposition that 'Countries around the world should act as part of a global community that works together to solve problems', not 'independent nations that compete … and pursue their own interests', and clear majority (58 per cent) support for taking others' interests into account and compromising with them.[48] More specifically, Australian polling conducted by the Lowy Institute over the last fifteen years shows clear, and often overwhelming, public support for just about all the benchmark tests of good international citizenship I have identified in these pages.[49] Overseas aid at first sight seems the big exception, but on closer examination—as explained below—it is anything but that.

In the case of human rights, for example, when asked in 2012 about the importance of key UN-recognised universal rights, 99 per cent of Lowy's Australian respondents answered affirmatively for fair trial, 97 per cent for the right to vote, 98 per cent for free expression, and 85 per cent for media free of censorship, while in 2015 there was majority support (albeit narrow, at 51 per cent) for Australia playing an active role in pushing for the abolition of the death penalty internationally.

In the case of appropriate responses to conflict and mass atrocity crimes, there has been strong support expressed for Australian military forces assisting in other parts of the world. In 2005, 91 per cent agreed with our participation in UN or regionally organised peacekeeping operations; 84 per cent agreed this was appropriate to prevent genocide or gross abuse of human rights on the scale of Rwanda, Kosovo or Sudan; and 82 per cent supported such operations if asked by a friendly country in our neighbourhood to prevent an internal collapse. In 2011, 82 per cent were in favour of UN-authorised military intervention 'in situations like Libya … to try to stop the government attacking its own citizens', and in 2019, 77 per cent favoured sending Australian forces to restore law and order in a Pacific nation.

When it comes to asylum seekers, much depends on the way the question is asked. General support is evident for strong border-protection measures, with 74 per cent expressing concern in 2013 about unauthorised boat arrivals, only 45 per cent in 2016 agreeing that Australia was a wealthy country which should accept more refugees, and only 28 per cent in 2019 thinking tough government policies hurt Australia's reputation. But when questions are more specifically framed, more compassion and tolerance is evident. In 2016, 62 per cent agreed the government was right to resettle 12 000 Syrian refugees, and 65 per cent thought it was wrong to favour Christians and other religions over Muslims in our refugee intake. And support levels are even higher when people are confronted with the plight of particular individuals: around 85 per cent in the case of the Biloela family.[50]

In the case of pandemics, the only questions in Lowy polling about Australia's international responsibilities were asked in 2021, in the context of the COVID-19 crisis, when there was a big majority—83 per cent—supporting aid for Pacific island countries to buy vaccines, and 60 per cent support for similar assistance in South-East Asia. On climate change, by contrast, there has been regular Lowy polling since 2006, with a fairly constant proportion of respondents—hovering around 60 per cent—agreeing that global warming is a serious and pressing problem, and that we should be taking steps now to address it even if this involves significant costs. Gaps are evident between the responses here of younger and older, and city and regional, Australians, but they are beginning to narrow.

Attitudes to nuclear weapons have again been polled only rarely by the Lowy Institute, but the answers on the record offer little solace to true believers in their desirability. In 2009, 75 per cent agreed that global nuclear disarmament should be a top priority for the Australian Government, while a year later, when asked 'If some of Australia's near neighbours were to begin to develop nuclear weapons, would you personally be in favour or against Australia also developing nuclear weapons?', 84 per cent of respondents said no.

But how does all that stand up when one focuses on policies and programs that might impact more directly on people's hip-pocket nerves? What about overseas aid in particular? Isn't it the case that in Australia, as elsewhere, public opinion surveys reinforce the argument that it's not just governments but ordinary people who are driven by the notion that charity begins at home? When the then Australian minister for international development stated in 2018 that '80 per cent of Australians do not support any further increase in foreign aid', wasn't she in fact relying on a 2017 Lowy Institute Poll to that effect?[51]

But survey questions can sometimes conceal more than they reveal. The 2017 Lowy Poll, which actually recorded 73 per cent of respondents describing Australia's aid as too much or about right, prefaced its question by telling respondents that the current aid budget was $3.8 billion. When its researchers revisited the question the following year, they took a different approach. Instead of stating a dollar amount for the current program, they asked respondents what percentage of the national budget they thought we should be spending on overseas development assistance. It turned out—and this is consistent with research findings elsewhere about public attitudes to foreign aid—that average Australians had a wildly inflated perception of the size of the program. They believed it constituted about 14 per cent of the federal budget and should be capped at a lower level, about 10 per cent—that is, at $10 rather than $14 of every $100 spent. But in reality aid's actual proportion of the budget was at the time just 0.8 per cent, or 80 cents in every $100 spent. The arithmetic is revealing: people thought we invested seventeen-and-a-half times the amount we actually did, and were happy for us to be twelve-and-a-half times more generous than we actually were![52]

That generosity of sentiment, it is important to appreciate, reflects what we also know about the compassion and generosity of ordinary Australians when it comes to themselves actually donating to international humanitarian causes. After the Indian Ocean tsunami on Boxing Day 2004 devastated communities around the region, while the Australian Government donated $60 million for disaster relief, the contribution from the general public through NGOs was $330 million! Australians are as compassionate as anyone else in the world when their attention is engaged on these issues.

It is hard to resist the conclusion that if Australia over the years has been much less consistently and effectively a good international citizen than it could have been, when measured against the benchmarks I have described, the problem lies not with the negative attitudes of our people, but our governments. Those in office might prefer Berthold Brecht's solution—'Dissolve the people and elect another'—but the right course for the rest of us is to persuade our political leaders, on both moral and national interest grounds, to change their ways, and vote them out if they don't. When governments have taken strongly principled good international citizenship positions, they have had no obvious difficulty in taking the community with them. The nervousness so many of them have shown has not had any obvious political justification. Maybe these issues are not sufficiently central and salient to win elections, but there is no evidence of which I am aware that they lose them.

It is also hard to resist the conclusion—whatever one's biases (and of course I acknowledge that mine are pro-Labor)—that over the decades since World War II, ALP governments have been far more instinctively inclined than their Coalition counterparts to embrace and implement good international citizenship principles, even if some of them have been rather more timid, and not only on overseas aid, than they needed to be. While not all Labor governments—or Labor governments in waiting—can be described as 'enlargers', and by no means all Tories have been 'straiteners', to apply Manning Clark's immortal distinction, pursuing 'purposes beyond ourselves' just does seem to be part of the party's DNA in a way which is not obvious in its opponents. Alison Pert's very academically stringent book-length analysis of *Australia as a Good International Citizen* draws conclusions to the same effect.[53] For both of us, the stand-out periods were Dr Evatt's tenure as foreign minister, the Whitlam government, the Hawke–Keating governments, and the first Rudd government.

At the core of the difference has been the instinctive attachment of Labor governments to multilateral institutions and processes, one usually not shared by their Coalition opponents, although there have been exceptions like Malcolm Fraser, whose passion for the Commonwealth in particular knew no bounds. They are far more likely to find common ground with US Republicans like former secretary of state James Baker, to whom I once said in semi-jest, 'The trouble with you Americans, Jim, is that you have a reflexive prejudice against the UN.' To which his reply, not entirely tongue-in-cheek, was, 'No, Gareth, it's not a reflexive prejudice. It's a considered prejudice.'

Looking forward, what can be done to persuade Australian policymakers to be more consistently committed to pursuing good international citizenship objectives? What can be done to encourage Coalition policymakers to be at least as consistently engaged as the Labor Party has been over the decades in advancing these causes, and in particular for the Liberal Party to rediscover in this context some of its liberal, not just conservative, traditions? What can be done to encourage my Labor colleagues to be less cautious than they too often have been when it comes to giving real practical content to the party's traditional liberal internationalist and humanitarian instincts? And how can the corner parties and independents, who have so often held the balance of legislative power in the Australian Parliament in recent times, be encouraged to exercise that power productively?

If we are to make progress on these fronts, I think those of us trying to make it happen—whether we are in politics ourselves, or government service, the media, academia, the think-tank and NGO world, or anywhere else—have to harness both the power of emotion and the power of reason.

Harnessing the power of emotion means, when it comes to taking action on good international citizenship benchmark issues, recognising and playing much more confidently to the inherent decency of ordinary Australians—decency for which there is ample hard evidence, if such is needed, in the opinion polls just cited. It means recognising that most Australians do want to do the right thing, even if at some cost to themselves, when it comes to overseas aid, responding to mass atrocity crimes, rescuing people from the scourge of war, saving future generations from existential risk and all the rest. It means that, whatever the foundations of the morality that moves them—be it religious, humanistic, or stemming from some other cultural or philosophical roots—good international citizenship is indeed a moral imperative for most people most of the time, although they may never have thought about things in these terms.

Recognising and appealing to people's moral instincts and emotions does not mean that it is ever very sensible, if one wants one's country to be a better international citizen, to be too absolutist in the positions one advocates. I don't think I have ever been quite as cynically pragmatic as my friend and former colleague James Baker—to quote him again—when he memorably said to me once, in the context of an argument we were having about nuclear disarmament, 'Well sometimes,

Gareth, you just have to rise above principle.' But tough compromise choices are sometimes inevitable in public policymaking if you want to be productive, not unproductive or—worse—counterproductive.

The biggest risk for idealists in this context is making the best the enemy of the good—insisting on an ideal but unachievable solution to a problem, and in the process ending up with something worse. It is extraordinary how often this risk has been ignored in recent Australian history, nowhere more damagingly—it has to be said again—than with the failure to gain parliamentary majorities for the Rudd government's CPRS in 2009 and the Gillard government's 'Malaysian solution' for offshore processing of refugees in 2012. Neither were perfect solutions, but both were infinitely preferable to the policies they failed to replace, in both cases because the Australian Greens allowed their idealism to completely override their rational judgement.[54]

Harnessing the power of reason means not just recognising the point just made—namely, that if progress is to be made, and counterproductive outcomes avoided, emotion sometimes has to be moderated by reason. More than that, it means, in the present context, making the case for a state being a good international citizen on a completely different basis than an appeal to emotion or moral instinct. It means arguing, rather, that such an approach is just as much a hard-headed *national interest*, for all the reasons spelt out earlier in these pages, as the traditional duo of security and economic interests on which governments have traditionally focused. I suspect the real utility of such advocacy is not so much with the wider population, although certainly there it constitutes a useful additional selling point, supplementing simple appeals to decency. Rather, its primary utility will be with those cynically inclined politicians, advisers and public servants who are themselves rather immune to moral arguments, particularly if they impact budget bottom lines, and who find it difficult to believe that anything other than appeals to self-interest can ever be widely supported in the community.

Nobody, least of all me, suggests that viewing foreign policymaking through the lens of good international citizenship is going to provide anything like all the answers we need in wrestling with complex problems of the kind I have been discussing. But it does give us, I believe, a much more helpful framework for dealing with the complexities of the highly interdependent world of the twenty-first century—with its multitude of transnational issues only capable of being solved by cooperative multilateralism—than an approach which focuses almost wholly on traditional, narrowly defined, security and economic interests.

Focusing attention on what it means to be, and be seen to be, a good international citizen also sets us a challenge. A country with Australia's general record and reputation as an energetic, creative middle power which has on many occasions in the past played a world-leading role in international diplomacy—in institution building, and on peace and security and other issues—ought perhaps to be setting its sights rather higher. We should be acting more generously than we have tended to in recent times towards those who share our common humanity around the world. We can only hope that this is a challenge to which all sides of politics can now rise. The bottom line is that we have just one planet, we are a global community, and our political leaders should give more weight than too many of them have done to what Abraham Lincoln famously called 'the better angels of our nature'.

My argument throughout this essay has been that there are two big reasons why we should care that Australia is, and is seen to be, a good international citizen—not just because it is the right thing for us to do morally, but because it is also in our national self-interest. If our political leaders think that being simultaneously idealistic and pragmatic is too complicated a story for them to tell, they should be reminded of Jimmy Maxton's famous admonition as a Scottish Labour MP in the 1930s: 'If you can't ride two horses at once, you've no right to be in the bloody circus.'

NOTES

1 Gareth Evans, 'Australia's Place in the World: The Dynamics of Foreign Policy Decision-Making', ANU, 6 December 1988, published as 'Making Australian Foreign Policy', Australian Fabian Society Pamphlet, no. 50, 1989; 'Australian Foreign Policy: Priorities in a Changing World', *Australian Journal of International Affairs*, vol. 43, no. 2, 1989, pp. 1–15.

2 On role models, see, for example, Geoffrey Stokes, Roderic Pitty and Gary Smith (eds), *Global Citizens: Australian Activists for Change*, Cambridge University Press, Melbourne, 2008; on education, see Gareth Evans, 'Purposes Beyond Ourselves: Educating for Global Citizenship', Indiana University address, 17 May 2015, http://www.gevans.org/speeches/speech571.html

3 Alison Pert, *Australia as a Good International Citizen*, The Federation Press, Sydney, 2014, p. 4, quoting Rt Hon Roland Michener.

4 For example, Nicholas J Wheeler and Tim Dunne, 'Good International Citizenship: A Third Way for British Foreign Policy', *International Affairs*, vol. 74, no. 4, 1998, pp. 847–70.

5 Alison Pert, *Australia as a Good International Citizen*, The Federation Press, Sydney, 2014; Gabriele Abbondanza, 'Australia the Good International Citizen? The Limits of a Traditional Middle Power', *Australian Journal of International Affairs*, vol. 75, no. 2, 2021, pp. 178–96. See also Peter Singer and Tom Gregg, *How Ethical Is Australia? An Examination of Australia's Record as a Global Citizen*, Australian Collaboration/Black Inc., Melbourne, 2004: Singer and Gregg focus on Australia's aid, trade, environment and refugees policies, and commitment to the UN.

6 Several sections of this book, especially those on Australia's record on, and my own policy approach as foreign minister towards, aid, human rights, conflict and atrocity prevention, and nuclear disarmament, draw directly from my previous published writing, notably Gareth Evans, *Incorrigible Optimist: A Political Memoir*, Melbourne University Press, Melbourne, 2017, chs 4–9.

7 Derek Parfit, *On What Matters*, Oxford University Press, Oxford, 2013, quoted in Peter Singer, *Ethics in the Real World*, Text, Melbourne, 2016, p. 8.

8 In September 2021 Singer was awarded the Berggruen Prize for Philosophy and Culture, worth US$1 million, which he promptly announced he would give away in its entirety to support global poverty reduction and animal rights.

9 My philosopher friend Peter Singer reminds me that, for him and other utilitarians going back to Bentham and Mill, our common *humanity* is not morally decisive: what matters is being sentient, having the capacity to suffer or enjoy life, and in that context our moral obligations extend to non-human animals. Being more of a utilitarian than a Kantian myself, I fully accept his point, and can see its relevance in international policy contexts like whaling and the protection of endangered species. But, in making the case here for good international citizenship as a moral imperative, I see Singer's position not as undermining my reliance on the centrality of our common humanity, but as adding another dimension to it.

10 See Joseph S Nye, 'Soft Power: The Evolution of a Concept', *Journal of Political Power*, vol. 14, no. 1, 2021, pp. 196–208.

11 'True Believer: The FP Interview', *Foreign Policy*, March–April 2001, p. 29.

12 The 0.7 per cent ODA/GNP (gross national product) target, originally recommended by the 1969 Pearson Commission *Partners in Development* report, was adopted by the UN General Assembly and OECD in 1970, and has been endorsed since by multiple international organisations and conferences, including the EU, G8 and UN World Summit. GNP was replaced by GNI, essentially the same concept, following the adoption of the revised System of National Accounts in 1993.

13 Stephen Howes, 'Australia Hits (Almost) Rock Bottom in New Global Aid Rankings', *Devpolicy Blog*, ANU, 10 May 2021, https://devpolicy.org/australia-hits-almost-rock-bottom-in-new-global-aid-rankings-20210510-2; also see his Australian Aid Tracker, https://devpolicy.org/aidtracker/comparisons. See also Micah, 'Australian Aid', 2021, https://www.micahaustralia.org/agency/australian_aid

14 Alison Pert (*Australia as a Good International Citizen*, The Federation Press, Sydney, 2014) offers good narrative descriptions of Australia's aid performance for different periods at pp. 95–6 (1941–72), 114, 122–3 (1972–83), 149–50 (1983–96), 179–80 (1996–2007) and 199–200 (2007–13).

15 Robin Davies, 'Measuring Australia's Foreign Aid Generosity, from Menzies to Turnbull', ANU Policy Development Centre, Policy Brief 16, February 2017, https://devpolicy.org/publications/policy_briefs/PB16%20Measuring%20Australia%E2%80%99s%20foreign%20aid%20generosity.pdf

16 Department of Foreign Affairs and Trade, 'In the National Interest', white paper, 1997, quoted in Peter Singer and Tom Gregg, *How Ethical Is Australia? An Examination of Australia's Record as a Global Citizen*, Australian Collaboration/Black Inc., Melbourne, 2004, p. 17.

17 Professor Stephen Howes, Director, Development Policy Centre, ANU, email to the author, 13 May 2021.

18 The following account draws on the helpful narrative descriptions in Alison Pert, *Australia as a Good International Citizen*, The Federation Press, Sydney, 2014, at pp. 88–90, 96–101 (1941–72), 108–10, 119–20 (1972–83), 130–41 (1983–96), 158–65 (1996–2007), 189–90 (2007–13) and 213–14.

19 Gareth Evans and Bruce Grant, *Australia's Foreign Relations*, 2nd edn, Melbourne University Press, Melbourne, 1995, p. 156.

20 Gareth Evans, *Cooperating for Peace: The Global Agenda for the 1990s and Beyond*, Allen & Unwin, Sydney, 1993.

21 For a full account of the Cambodian peace process and its aftermath, see Gareth Evans, *Incorrigible Optimist: A Political Memoir*, Melbourne University Press, Melbourne, 2017, pp. 152–9.

22 The figures here are from Australian War Memorial, 'Australians and Peacekeeping', 2021, https://www.awm.gov.au/articles/peacekeeping, and RAMSI's website (https://www.ramsi.org). For a detailed account of some of these operations, see the volumes so far published in the Australian War Memorial's *Official History of Peacekeeping, Humanitarian and Post-Cold War Operations*, including the—aptly titled—vol. III, *The Good International Citizen: Australian Peacekeeping in Asia, Africa and Europe 1991–93*, Cambridge University Press, Melbourne, 2014.

23 See Steven Bullard, *In Their Time of Need: Australia's Overseas Emergency Relief Operations 1918–2006*, vol. VI, *Official History of Peacekeeping, Humanitarian and Post-Cold War Operations*, Cambridge University Press, Melbourne, 2017; launched by Gareth Evans: see 'Australia's Humanitarian Peacekeepers', http://www.gevans.org/speeches/Speech636.html

24 I am indebted to the ANU's David Horner for extracting this information for me from the impenetrable Defence Department website. The deployments are to UNMISS (up to twenty ADF personnel), MFO (up to twenty-seven), UNTSO (twelve) and MINUSMA (one staff officer).

25 For a full discussion of all these legal and moral issues, see Gareth Evans, 'When Is It Right to Fight? Legality, Legitimacy and the Use of Military Force', Cyril Foster Lecture, Oxford University, May 2004, published in *Survival*, vol. 46, no. 3, 2004, pp. 59–81, http://www.gevans.org/speeches/speech105.html

26 See Gareth Evans, 'The Real Risks of Australia's Submarine Deal', distributed worldwide by Project Syndicate, 22 September 2021, and published in the *Australian Financial Review*, 24 September 2021.

27 For a detailed account of the background to, and early evolution of, R2P, see Gareth Evans, *The Responsibility to Protect: Ending Mass Atrocity Crimes Once and for All*, Brookings Institution Press, Washington, DC, 2008. For a more recent stocktake of its impact and prospects, see Gareth Evans, 'The Responsibility to Protect: The Dream and the Reality', Leeds University lecture, 26 November 2020, http://www.gevans.org/speeches/Speech721.html. There is now a large body of literature on this subject.

28 Department of Home Affairs, 'About the Refugee and Humanitarian Program', 24 February 2021, https://immi.homeaffairs.gov.au/what-we-do/refugee-and-humanitarian-program/about-the-program

29 In the brief account below of the historical record, I have drawn particularly from Alison Pert, *Australia as a Good International Citizen*, The Federation Press, Sydney, 2014, at pp. 90–91 (1941–72), 110–11, 120-1 (1972–83), 141–4 (1983–96), 162–4, 167-8 (1996–2007), 192–5 (2007–13) and 214.

30 Parliamentary Library Research Paper, 'Seeking Asylum: Australia's Humanitarian Program', 21 January 2011, https://www.aph.gov.au/About_Parliament/Parliamentary_Departments/Parliamentary_Library/pubs/BN/1011/SeekingAsylum. This paper usefully describes the complex definitional and operational issues involved in distinguishing between refugees, asylum seekers and those otherwise eligible for humanitarian entry, and onshore and offshore processing.

31 Behrouz Boochani, *No Friend But the Mountains: Writing from Manus Prison*, Picador Australia, Sydney, 2018, described at https://en.wikipedia.org/wiki/No_Friend_But_the_Mountains; on the Biloela family, see, for example, John Menadue, 'Moral Bankruptcy and Cruelty in the Treatment of the Biloela Family', *Pearls and Irritations*, 17 June 2021, and for general background, see https://en.wikipedia.org/wiki/Murugappan_family_asylum_claims

32 Peter Mares, 'A Line in the Water', *Inside Story*, 28 August 2021, quoting Madeleine Gleeson and Natasha Yaccoub, *Cruel, Costly and Ineffective: The Failure of Offshore Processing in Australia*, Policy Brief 11, The Kaldor Centre for International Refugee Law, UNSW, August 2021.

33 Abul Rizvi, 'Blink and the Boats Will Restart the Government Says, But that Is Nonsense', *Pearls and Irritations*, 16 June 2021; '*The Australian* Again Falls for Government Spin on the Record Number of Asylum Seekers Arriving by Air', *Pearls and Irritations*, 30 January 2020.

34 Eliza Mackintosh, 'A Band-Aid over a Gaping Hole', *CNN*, 8 August 2021, https://edition.cnn.com/2021/08/07/world/covid-vaccine-booster-shot-inequality-intl-gbr-cmd/index.html

35 See Deborah Gleeson, 'Australia Has Finally Backed a Plan to Let Developing Countries Make Cheap COVID-19 Vaccines', *The Conversation*, 14 September 2021.

36 See Alyssia Leng and Roland Rajah, 'Assessing Australia's Role in Global Vaccine Equity', *The Interpreter*, Lowy Institute, 25 October 2021; Hilary Mansour, 'Australia Needs to Step Up as PNG Is Hit by COVID', *The Age*, 18 October 2021.

37 See, for example, 2021 Lowy Institute Poll, summarised by Daniel Hurst, 'Seven in 10 Australians Want Government to Take More Action on Climate, Survey Finds', *The Guardian*, 26 May 2021, https://www.theguardian.com/environment/2021/may/26/seven-in-10-australians-want-government-to-take-more-action-on-climate-survey-finds

38 For example, Jennifer Hewett, 'The PM's "Magic Pudding" Climate Plan', *Australian Financial Review*, 27 October 2021.

39 See Michael Mazengarb, 'Australia Ranked Dead Last in World for Climate Action in Latest UN Report', *Renew Economy*, 1 July 2021, https://reneweconomy.com.au/australia-ranked-dead-last-in-world-for-climate-action-in-latest-un-report; see https://www.sdgindex.org/reports/sustainable-development-report-2021 for full text of the report.

40 See Ross Gittins, 'PM Can't See the Emissions Truth for the Trees', *The Age*, 13 August 2021, https://www.theage.com.au/business/the-economy/pm-can-t-see-the-emissions-truth-for-the-trees-20210812-p58ibc.html

41 See Wesley Morgan, 'Ripple Effect: The Cost of Our Pacific Neglect', *Australian Foreign Affairs*, vol. 12, 2021, pp. 30–48.

42 Ross Garnaut, *Superpower: Australia's Low Carbon Opportunity*, Black Inc., Melbourne, 2019, quoted in Amanda McKenzie, 'Towards Glasgow: Why Australia's Climate Policy Is Risking Our Future', *Australian Foreign Affairs*, vol. 12, 2021, pp. 69–88, at p. 80.

43 On nuclear risks generally, see the Chatham House Report, 'Too Close for Comfort: Cases of Near Nuclear Use and Options for Policy', Royal Institute of International Affairs, April 2014; and on nuclear winter, see Alan Robock and Owen Brian Toon, 'Self-Assured Destruction: The Climate Impacts of Nuclear War', *Bulletin of the Atomic Scientists*, vol. 68, no. 5, 2012, pp. 66–74.

44 For the '2021 Doomsday Clock Statement', see https://thebulletin.org/doomsday-clock/current-time

45 On the global nuclear arsenal in 2021, see Federation of American Scientists, 'Status of World Nuclear Forces', 2021, https://fas.org/issues/nuclear-weapons/status-world-nuclear-forces

46 See Department of Foreign Affairs and Trade, *Report of the Canberra Commission on the Elimination of Nuclear Weapons*, Canberra, 1996; and International Commission on Nuclear Non-Proliferation and Disarmament, *Eliminating Nuclear Threats: A Practical Agenda for Global Policymakers*, Canberra/Tokyo, 2009.

47 The 1995 ICJ advisory opinion on Legality of the Threat or Use of Nuclear Weapons is at https://www.icj-cij.org/en/case/95; for my statement as counsel for Australia in support of illegality, see https://www.gevans.org/speeches/old/1995/301095_case_illegality.pdf

48 James Bell et al., 'International Cooperation Welcomed across 14 Advanced Economies', Pew Research Center, 21 September 2020, https://www.pewresearch.org/global/2020/09/21/international-cooperation-welcomed-across-14-advanced-economies

49 The Lowy Institute in Sydney has been annually tracking public opinion on major current foreign policy issues since 2005: see https://www.lowyinstitute.org/about/programs-and-projects/polling. Different questions are asked each year—comprehensively tabulated at https://poll.lowyinstitute.org/charts/#section-themes—which make for snapshots, as with those in my text, rather than easy comparisons over time. But the overall pattern of responses on particular issues is consistent.

50 Rebecca Magro, 'Australians Want the Murugappan Family Returned to Biloela', *Hunter and Bligh*, 17 June 202, https://www.hunterandbligh.com.au/hb-insights/australians-want-the-murugappan-family-returned-to-biloela; *The Canberra Times*, '"Biloela Family" Deserves Compassion', 15 June 2021, https://www.canberratimes.com.au/story/7296192/biloela-family-deserves-compassion

51 Minister Concetta Fierravanti-Wells at the Overseas Development Institute, London, reported by Latika Bourke, 'Australians Don't Want to Spend More on Foreign Aid, Admits Minister',

The Sydney Morning Herald, 17 April 2018, https://www.smh.com.au/politics/federal/australians-don-t-want-to-spend-more-on-foreign-aid-admits-minister-20180417-p4z9zi.html. For the 2017 Lowy Institute Poll, which found that 73 per cent thought the current aid budget of approximately $3.8 billion was either 'about the right amount' or 'too much'—a response almost identical to that in 2015 when the aid budget was $5 billion (over 30 per cent higher)—see https://www.lowyinstitute.org/publications/2017-lowy-institute-poll. See also Terence Wood, 'Aid Policy and Australian Public Opinion', *Asia and the Pacific Policy Studies*, vol. 5 no. 2, 2018, pp. 235–48.

52 For the 2018 Lowy Institute Poll, see https://www.lowyinstitute.org/publications/2018-lowy-institute-poll; and for a discussion of its implications, see Jonathan Pryke, 'New Research Shows Australians Have Wrong Idea on Foreign Aid Spending', *The Conversation*, 26 June 2018.

53 See Gareth Evans, 'Enlargers, Straiteners and the Making of Australian Foreign Policy', *Meanjin Quarterly*, vol. 70 , no. 2, 2011, pp. 124–32; Alison Pert, *Australia as a Good International Citizen*, The Federation Press, Sydney, 2014, pp. 216–17.

54 See John Menadue, 'Australia Paying a Heavy Price for Greens Purity', *Crikey*, 27 June 2012.

IN THE NATIONAL INTEREST

Other books on the issues that matter: